The Spiritual Heartache

by

Hamza S. Khan

AF520033

Double 9 BOOKS

The Spiritual Heartache

by Hamza S. Khan

Copyright © 2024

All Rights reserved.

No part of this publication may be reproduced, stored in a retrieval system, or transmitted in any form or by any means, electronic, mechanical, photocopying or Otherwise, without the written permission of the publisher.
The author/editor asserts the moral right to be identified as the author/editor of this work.

ISBN: 978-93-64280-95-2

Published by

DOUBLE 9 BOOKS
2/13-B, Ansari Road
Daryaganj, New Delhi – 110002
info@double9books.com
www.double9books.com
Tel. 011-40042856

ABOUT THE AUTHOR

"The Spiritual Heartache" is a captivating novel penned by Hamza Salim Khan, a dedicated student who is currently immersed in the study of Forensic Science in Sandip University. Alongside his academic endeavors, Hamza's creative mind brims with enchanting love stories, evocative poems, insightful quotes, and heart-stirring poetries.

He has written many stories since childhood but never published.

His passion for writing has led him to contribute five poignant poems to various anthologies, and he continues to share his evocative poetry through his Instagram account.

This novel stands as a significant milestone in Hamza's life, marking his debut as a published author.

The double 9 book publication gave me the strength to publish a big size of the book. Also, my friends and sisters encouraged me to publish the book after reading my stories, quotes, and poems.

CONTENTS

Author's notes

Love is a flame that burns bright.

In this book, I have explained what is the status of love in the eyes of God.

Sahih al-Bukhari is a collection of hadith compiled by Muhammad al Bukhari. I have taken most of the lessons from this book.

Many stories of the Islamic religion explained to us the meaning of Love.

There would be a large number of Muslim or non-Muslim readers here. . But, some of those who didn't hear they may have built curiosity in reading.

I am publishing the love genre for the first time. I am not an expert writer, nor am I a seasoned writer in any sense. I have lots of stories, but I haven't written this big size from the book.

I am a co-author of the books of

Inked by heart

Ehsas: ek shayar ka

Wisdom and Words

Season of the Eternal Love

The wordy tales

Which are available on Amazon.

I am not only just part of the book. I have many supporters who supported me and Dragged it here.

Everyone says that a woman is responsible for a man's success. Whether she is your sister, friend, or wife. I have two friends: Isha Parkhe and Janhavi Korde. s who encouraged me to publish this novel.

Rashika Rangari and Rahila Khan, my friend always admired my work and encouraged my every work.

I create love sagas in my mind and make them the best. Also, I took reference to hadith and Islamic stories which were taught to me by my sister Huma Khan.

Bismillah (Beginning)

Beneath the earth or above the sky, I found myself in a place where darkness pervaded, where there was no negativity, but the only deity was the power of love, and I could see one lady, the entire universe in the girl. She came to me and spoke out my name, "Daksh!"

"Daksh! Are you fine?" Ayan worriedly waking up me.

I got up and I saw my friends around us. And I was being located at the portico of the train.

The train was rushing from the dense forest when the sun had already set, and dusk was spreading.

The train was running at a good time. My days were going to change forever. I was the best person among them and will come to be the poorest of them. I figured out the significance of Vitality is that it is just a concert where every person in the world encounters many things, and some of them leave that many things by committing suicide. I wish this second option had been decided on. But, I had vowed her that I would never suicide. She elucidated everything about suicide. We didn't know the world after death. Suicide is the easiest word in the world and we consider it peace.

Peace is the word in the world and we feel it hereafter.

Were my friends who were very eager after meeting for a long time.

We traveled for 7 hours. Now, it was going to be completed in a total of 8 hours.

And then, Ramgarh arrived.

It was 8 O'Clock, and Sanchit had come for pick up. "Ananya, Vivek, Ayan, Pranjal, Shiva, Manasi," and sought my name. "Daksh, I thought you wouldn't come, but you came for…" he said in an excited voice.

I hugged him and said, "My brother's wedding is … How can I not come to my brother's wedding?" I hugged him. We had an ambivalent but now it would be fine. He tapped his tears.

"He is my younger brother, Anuj," Sanchit introduced his brother wiping his face.

"Anita?"

We fell silent.

He broke the silence and said to Anuj, "Daksh was my roommate."

Anuj nodded and opened the Scorpio's door, "Come, Let's go now,"

There were still four days remaining for the wedding. We went there to attend the wedding. But I didn't know that these turns could change my life again.

We reached Sanchit's house, and it was well-decorated with lights and flowers. Sanchit's parents welcomed us and showed us our rooms.

For Ananya, Pranjal, and Manasi, they showed one room, and for us, they showed a different one.

There was no bed, but they gave us a quilt for sleep.

We took a shower and went for dinner.

"You all guys remembered, when we were in our MBA how much we did joy together." Ananya giggled.

"Yeah, it was you that going to make us fool and you made only in front of that Hitler." Sanchit pointed to Ananya.

"Hitler..." Manasi chided after hearing his name. "I hate that person. He was something irritating in the name of teacher."

We laughed. "Here take it chicken leg piece, don't chide." Sanchit chuckled.

As we met after a long time, we all were talking about our pasts.

"Aisha?" Sanchit asked.

I paused my laughing and rolled down my eyes.

All were silent and Sanchit offered dal, "Hmm, here take it."

We finished our dinner. And sat it on the sofa for some time. Sanchit stood and said, "Come on let's go for sleep now. You all may tired."

"Yes, Good night guys!" Pranjal greeted.

"Good night," all the others said in Chorus to each other.

We all went to sleep. We all slept.

Suddenly, I woke up at midnight. Cold breezes were passing through the balcony.

I went to the balcony of the room to close the door.

It was a cold night, and The cold wind was swinging the curtains. Stars were visible in the sky. I saw outside forests and trees were spread till the end of the land. There was one beautiful river, which I couldn't see because of the low height of the bungalow. I heard a car's voice.

I saw one girl who was entering from the gate, and Sanchit and his family were welcoming her. Her ear reflection was disturbing my eyes, and I was unable to see her. She wrote down to the house. After some minutes, I went outside for searching the water.

I heard a crying girl. Maybe she was that girl who entered the house some minutes ago. I thought that I should go, but I did not change positions. Her crying voice attracted me. And that voice seemed somewhat friendly. There was too much inquisitiveness to see who is she.

I had lost my sleep that night.

Next morning,

I was thinking about the same girl. I took a shower, and I came out with a wrapping towel on my waist. I got ready and I walked down to the living room, and there were the families assembled, and they were jabbering.

I was trying to find her, but I couldn't recognize her. I was trying to spot her earrings which were shining last night.

Suddenly, I heard Anklet's voice, and with the tackling of empty cups.

She put the empty cup tray on the table, poured it into tea, and served it to each of the other family. I stood in the passage and watched her doing this. She was coming back after served tea. There's the way to the kitchen through the passage. She saw me while going on her way.

She looked at me. "Tea?" I asked arching one eyebrow.

She looked at the tray in her hand.

Her beautiful voice killed me, "Oh, Sorry, this is all over. Wait, let me bring."

I said, "Oh, It's okay… No need."

"But why, I wanted to."

"Oh, then you can," I grinned.

"Wait… I will bring it for you" She chuckled.

It was an awkward moment with her when guests were watching us.

I followed her to the kitchen.

"It smells so good."

"Oye, the mister, don't try to flirt with me."

"Why do you feel that I am teasing you."

"You followed me till the kitchen."

"Yeah, I just want your tricks to make tea; it smells so good. What will happen to me if I drink? "

"Nothing! And why do you want to make tea." Closed her half eyes and asked.

"If my wife will come to my house, then I will also offer her such good smells tea."

"Wow, You city people are amazing and so helpful, right? I like helping his wife with household work."

"So, please like me too because I will help her so much if she comes." I chuckled.

And I stood there till the tea was completely made.

"Go now!" She insisted.

"But I don't want to." I joked.

"Okay, meet me this evening outside the gate; you are very interesting."

"Seriously! " I arched one eyebrow.

"Go now, and this is not your Mumbai where a boy and girl can talk openly like this. This is Ramgarh of Uttar Pradesh, and the people are too possessive. And this is a village." She pushed me out of the kitchen.

I went to my room, and there Ayan said, "Where were you?"

I asked, "Who is that girl, the one who was serving tea!"

"Oh wow… What a Choice," Pranjal said teasingly.

"Shut up, Pranjal. She is not my choice." I lied. "I promised after Krishna I don't want anyone."

"Oh, Brother, if you have any plan to propose to her, then please forget it. She is the sister of our friend Sanchit. And you know Sanchit, how is he?

He is too much possessive from college life. Remember that day? He fought many times for his girlfriend, Anita. She left him just because he was too possessive." Said Shiva.

"Forget it, guys; today, there is Sangeet we will enjoy." Excitedly Manasi.

It was evening; everyone was busy with the Sangeet ceremony. I went outside the gate, and then that girl came. I asked her, "Are you the sister of Sanchit."

"Yes, my name is Diya."

"Diya!! Nice name"

She said, "Shall we go to the river bank?"

"Yeah, sure, but what about the ceremony?"

"Leave! We will come by 6."

And we left for the river bank. It was 5:30 p.m. when the sun was setting off. We were riding in a boat. She had collected many stones with her.

She threw the pebble on the river, and it bounced 7-8 times on the surface of the river.

I said, "Please, I also want to do this."

She said, "Hold the stone and hold it from the index finger and thumb flatlet and throw."

I followed her, but I failed the first 4/5 times, and then it was working. And we both were playing stone-throwing wing on the river.

She paused playing and stared at me playing. And she was going to say something but suddenly she fell into the river.

I also jumped to save her.

I paused for a while; she was holding me. She put her hand on my back, her wet lips were touching my chest, and her wet hair was lying on my face. She held me, and instead of me saving her, she saved me. We held the boat and the boatman picked me up first and she was helping me to ascend. Then she came with herself.

We were completely wet. Boatmen took the boat to the riverside and we descended over there.

I took out my shirt and started squeezing it so that the shirt got dry. She was wearing a white suit. Due to getting wet, her whole body was visible. I offered her my shirt to wear, And when I went close to her to give her the shirt, she hugged me. And I also hugged her tightly, Slowly moved my lips closer to her throat, and started kissing her on her neck. She lay down on the bank of the river, and I lay on her. I was moving my hand from her waist, and then gradually, I was going up. Suddenly, I got the idea that she was her friend's sister. I stood up. And said, "See Diya, you are my friend's sister. I can't."

She said, "You know Daksh when Bhai showed us your pictures when he used to live in the hostel. I like you since then."

"What?"

"Yes, Daksh"

"Love's eternal flame is there in my heart for a long period. I was waiting for the moment to talk to you, to meet you… And Finally, you got me."

I was a bit confused at the time. She confessed, "I love you, Daksh."

Tears were continuously flowing, her moist eyes attracted me.

'Till now I have loved someone. But this time someone loved me. I leave everything to God. She had always explained to me that if you do not understand something then you should leave it to God. Of course, he knows everything. ' I thought.

I said, "I respect your feelings and I Love You too!"

She asked, "Do you believe in God."

I replied, "I didn't but I do now."

I kissed her on her forehead.

"I knew Daksh, if my feelings are true, then the feelings inside you will also emerge. And that's occurred," Diya said with rips in her eyes. I wiped the tears on her wet face with my thumb. "Diya, I am pleasing you, don't leave me. I have already broken." My words might touched her.

Only then did Sanchit and the rest reach there.

Sanchit saw me doing this. He came directly and hit me stiff on my face. And he crept Diya.

"Love is nothing but uncontrollable emotions and feelings."

Ceremony or Tragedy

Ceremony of Sangeet, People around me were happy, and all were enjoying the Sangeet. But I was scanning that Sanchit's mood was off. I sat and eyed the dance.

He was thinking something while standing, and he went up the stairs.

I don't know how I was attracted to her, even though I already had one girl whom I loved the most, and yes, she left me. Also, Diya loves me the most. I had already passed through the circumstances of break up, and I had promised myself that I would never be in any relationship. But, human nature, especially man's nature, is the same in that he changes his thoughts for the girl until he gets a good one.

I was still thinking of that girl at last twilight. My enthusiasm after listening to her familiar voice and her earrings reflected in my eyes. I saw her long black hair, which was tied from the back. Suddenly, I started thinking of Diya, whose hair, and beautiful eyes, where I drowned. I was hugging her and me...... Breaking the train of'thought after listening to the cheering of my friend Ayan. I saw Anaya, Pranjal, and Manasi hitting the dance floor. They were dancing, and I was searching her that earring girl by watching their dance. But in this open crowd, I couldn't find her.

And then I was finding Diya, and I could not find Diya.

Again I had thought of Sanchit while walking upstairs. He took me wrong. Of course, I made a mistake, but it's not just my mistake. Diya was attracting me towards herself. 'I shouldn't have attracted her' I regretted too. But she loves me, and do I? No... I love only a girl, but she is not with me. With these thousand thoughts, I went upstairs to prove myself right, and when I opened the door.

"Sanchit was tied from the fan," I said to the officer. Tears were continuously flowing from my eyes. I saw the officer he was suspecting other people. He was interrogating every person present in the ceremony.

I was just scared of Diya. If she told him about this evening, then the officer would doubt on me.

The officer inspected his mobile, and they got the last call from his bride. She called him.

Such a big mishap had occurred, but she was not visible.

I was afraid of all these situations. I also had fought with Sanchit, before the ceremony. I thought I should elope from here. But seeing the condition of Sanchit's parents, I didn't go.

The condition of his mother and father had deteriorated. I went to them and tried to console them. But where is the heart of mother and father stuck? In the happiness of their youth, they lost their child. We went to his parents, tried to console them and explained to them.

Ayan and I were explaining to the aunt sitting there. With us, there were also her family members trying to console her. I said to Ayan lowering my voice, "I'm coming back." I went from there. I was confused, where Diya is? She had not been there since the function had started.

On the day of the wedding preparations, they were preparing for the funeral.

The ornate house was being uprooted. When I woke up from there, his bride also came. She wept a little and tried to understand Aunty. Giving her some relief and then she got up from there for her house. She didn't even wait for Antim Sanskar.

After searching everywhere in the house, Diya didn't get it. Some girls were sitting and they were sobbing. Pranjal was there too. I went to her and called her. I asked Pranjal, "Where is Diya? Did you see her"

She was crying and too upset. She nodded that she didn't. She hugged me, and said, "He left us, Sanchit left us, Daksh." I kept her quiet. I remembered Aisha's words, "This is not in our hands, every person has to go back to his God. Indeed, the God's property goes back to his God."

Her words are gettingg understood, on my every path. What she said, what she was talking about, I got all those things.

I was very upset and was looking for her.

One by one, everyone was coming for the funeral.

I went upstairs and checked for her in her room, in the garden, and everywhere. She didn't get me. I went to her room again, and on looking closely, I found a note.

I read that page and only then went out to find her. I said to Vivek to come with me and told Ayan and Shiva to take care of Aunty and Uncle.

The night was about to set in, and the body had to be taken for the pyre to be lit.

In the shadow of a dark blue sky, we were finding Diya in shades of dense forest. There was darkness in the forest. I was still finding her with my all efforts. Long trees surrounded us and didn't let us find Diya.

We heard the siren of the police car, and the light of the vehicle was falling in front of our eyes. I couldn't be able to catch sight of who is he.

He was the officer who came for an investigation. The same officer asked, "What's the matter? We know that it is not suicide. It is murder. Sanchit's Father is a well-known personality in this village. That's why we don't take corpses for the post-mortem. He was refuting it. Alright, we know that this is murder."

I said, "Sir, in front of me, all these happened." There were lines on my forehead.

"See, a person whose marriage was there tomorrow is such a happy person; how can he suddenly commit Suicide, Say??" He stopped us.

"Sir, sometimes we don't know what is happening in someone's mind."

"You are his best friend, and you were the roommate of him, right?" He asked suspiciously.

"Yes! But I was his roommate only for 1 month."

"Still you must know."

I said, "See, we are finding Diya in this forest. Please, sir, help us or leave us. Let me find her."

"Who is she? And what is the relation between you and her?"

"There's no relation between us but she is Sanchit's sister, and I don't have any relationship with her!"

"Then, why are you finding her?" He suspiciously asked.

"Sir, because she was too worried and went outside, and She hasn't come yet. So we both came out to find her." We reassured.

"Okay, then!" The officer sat in the car. "Come with me. Let's find her," the investigator said.

He was driving and asked simultaneously, "Tell me, did Sanchit have any girlfriends in college life? And answer me in detail without hiding anything."

"Yes Sir, Ankita was his girlfriend. He loved her too much. But she left because he was very suspicious. When he saw Anita and his cousin's brother together, he whacked his brother. And beat him very poorly. He can't be able to walk now. He thought that she might change her boyfriend. After that incident, Ankita left him. But, Sanchit still had feelings for her. When I arrived in Ramgarh, he first asked about her only. He had some other plan with her to elope or something. I thought she was coming that night. Because I found her voice, but I couldn't be able to recognize her properly. She was crying. Maybe she also had feelings for him. But I don't think so. Because she filled hatred for him after that incident."

"You mean that yesterday she came here to Ramgarh?"

"Yes sir, It's my doubt."

"Why didn't you tell me earlier? What else are you hiding.?"

"Nothing, sir…!"

He saw me suspiciously, and then we all went to find her. L

When we were searching in the forest, we heard the voice of the breaking of branches.

Yet, I found her in the forest. She was trying to strangulate herself, but maybe the branch couldn't bear the heavy weight, so she fell.

She faints down. I took her in my arms and lay her down in the officer's car.

He started the car and turned the car towards the hospital.

That officer said, "Vivek, you go and inform them this is in her house that she found."

He stopped the car and went to his house. I, the officer, went towards the hospital. She was lying on my lap, and I tapped her cheeks, calling her name, "Diya, Diya…"

She didn't open her eyes. The car was running too fast.

We reached the hospital, and I admitted her to the ward of the hospital.

The doctor came and asked, "What happened to her?"

"She was trying to suicide."

The doctor said, "This is a police case; first, we have to inform the police."

"Police arrived with us, don't worry." I replied, "he is outside. If you want to talk, then you can talk with him."

And they took Diya into the casualty ward.

I was waiting in front of her when nurses and doctors were doing her treatment.

They left her after they put a syringe on her. She slept for some hours.

She opened her eyes after some time. Suddenly, the officer inspector started his interrogation. He asked, "Why were you trying to suicide?"

She didn't say a word and started crying. I was trying to weep her tears, but I was afraid of her.

I offered tissue paper, but she didn't accept. And said, "Bhai died because of me. I am the only reason behind his death."

The officer inquired, "Was there anything happened between both of you.?"

"Yes, he saw me...." My heartbeats were running so fast, and I was perspiring profusely.

Maybe she stopped because she was feeling ashamed, or I don't know, and maybe she was defending me. I took a deep breath, and I was going to tell her what Sanchit was hiding from their family. But, I wanted to say in the absence of the officer. But he stood on our head. Before I would say, she continued, "... He saw me while Daksh was kissing, and he was very angry at that time."

"So you are saying that you and Daksh are the reason behind his mental health and suicide," Inspector raised a question mistrustfully.

"Sir, My intention was not ..."

"You shut up!" The inspector shouted, so I stopped talking.

"No, not I. He did. He was forcing me for my consent." Diya lied and trapped me in the case of murder. I didn't know that accepting love is also a sin.

"Sir, she is lying ..."

Then he shouted, "You, Shut up!"

"Sir, I am accepting that Sanchit Caught us, but don't be assured, please he has many reasons for committing suicide." He didn't even take my one word to his ears and continued,

"I know that was the murder. And because of you, Diya was also going to kill herself."

" What the hell Diya, why are you lying!" I exclaimed to her.

"Sir, my condition getting worse, please sir! Let him quiet."

'The genuine cause of death is we humans ourselves.'

Dreadful Prison

"Duty is my priority I won't come right now." The officer ranted at her wife when she called him.

I was frightened by his voice. I didn't know if I would punished or not. He denied his call and stared at me.

I was thinking about his statement. I thought he knew how to read my mind and he replied my question was roaming in my mind. "According to section 306 of IPC, you will be punished with imprisonment for ten years. It is bailable. So if you want to do advocates, then your family can." And he put handcuffs on my hands. He took me with him without any other inquiry. He was dragging me from the hospital. Everybody was looking at me. I embarrassed. I sat in his jeep. He drove me to the police station.

And they put me in lock-up. The officer came after hours with Sanchit's father, and said, " You, the betrayer, police told to us, that you killed Sanchit. Why? What do you get by doing this?"

" Uncle, I don't kill him. They were trapping me.,"

That officer stood quietly, staring down at the floor.

I'm in miserable condition right now, or else I would have killed you.

" Uncle, ask to Diya! I'm not a sinner of Sanchit.,"

They didn't listen to my words. From the words of Sanchit's Dad, I got it that he was keeping a veil on his respect, which was destructed by me.

The day when the officer was screaming at her wife, telling her his priority was duty. Now, he kept silent after seeing the money of Sanchit's father. The corrupt officer.

I was in lock-up for three days. I was waiting every day for someone. And especially Diya.

So, I could tell her the truth about Sanchit. There were also other reasons for Suicide.

Every time, every second I was waiting for for her. Maybe, she didn't love me. Because love is for the pure soul. I had experienced love, where I didn't get my loved one, but the only destruction.

The love puts on us a hefty burden. Which is not easy to lift for a lifetime.

I was waiting for Diya. So that we can talk, I wouldn't took her name incase I would free. I would have kept her respect.

I didn't even have any food to eat. I slept in the lock-up. Mosquitoes were continuously biting me. I felt cold but they didn't offer me a blanket. I realized her words. "Love's identification is a pain in your life." Aisha my best friend. She taught me to live life again.

I forgot her. 'Every person who came into my life was with me for a short period. When she arrived in my life then every person was going to live with me for long periods.' I realized that she was worth it in my life. Before this time, I was the happiest person, and I had already broken the thousands of hearts. And I did not even realize it.

Once I realize, that she didn't accept me. So, I never tried it again. Now I started realizing each word and phrase. Her words and her lessons were important in my life.

They shifted me to Ramgarh District Jail.

It was not a good time, when my blood even not responding my any of my actions. I was waiting for my family where they would come and do some advocacy. I had promised myself that I would not be in any relationship; still, I broke my promise. I was wrong. My family didn't support me. Every day I was dying. I was finding my way to get out of this dreasful prison.

I have one friend in jail. Vinay Kumar was the author. He was allegedly trapped in the murder case. When he was writing one of his famous novels Murder Mystery. The real culprits, who were his assistants, followed his novel, and according to the novel, they murdered their enemy. And they trapped Vinay in this murder. All the witnesses and shreds of evidence were found against Vinay Kumar. So, he was stuck here in prison.

He was not only the author, but also he had completed a BA in Criminology. But, due to some physical health, he didn't approach the police.

Some people are innocent in the World, bearing the oppression in their lives. But, Aisha said once about themselves, "The world is the dreadful Prison for believers and the heaven for the non-believers like atheists."

Some of her words touched my heart like someone stabbed thorns in my chest and removed it back.

"I don't believe in God, and j don't want to be a believer. Because, if there is no such existence what we will do to perform blind rituals to none." I replied when Vinay was curious to know why I am an atheist.

"your point of view is absolutely fine, but believing in God makes peace to our hearts. Whether he exists or not, it doesn't matter. But, if believing in him gives you peace and a blissful life we should believe in him." Vinay replied.

We were talking then the topic changed to my love life. I narrated about Diya, then only Havildar came, it was 6:00 pm, and it was dinner time. I was walking with him for dinner. There was lots of noise from other prisoners who were eagerly waiting for dinner. Vinay asked, "Do you know about Diya? Does she love you now?" I had to listen carefully because there was a lot of noise around.

I said loudly to hear him properly, "I don't know. But I know one thing I will never face anyone in my family. And Diya! I don't love her. And I don't care whether she loves me or not." The prisoners were banging their plates loudly.

"No, brother, your priority is to meet your family first and..." then one of the prisoners pushed him by walking towards the dining table. Vinay pushed him back from his elbow.

I started, "Family! I don't want to see all of them. Already, I know how to face all the problems of the world without anyone. I will spend my whole life without anyone."

We stood in the queue for dinner where other people were fighting for standing first in the queue. It was my fifth day in on so, I got much information about this prison. I got to know that we should stand in a queue by fighting with others.

"Brother, it seems very easy, but it is not. It is very difficult to spend your life without anyone." He was talking while walking ahead in a queue.

I nodded. We both took the plate, and they put rice and dal, spinach, and chapati. Spinach vegetables had only water. Rock-type chapati they served. I was hungry, so I was just going to sit at my table, then one man pushed me, and all the vegetables, dal, and rice on the plate fell. I didn't have the strength to fight with him, so I left him. "You can eat from my plate. They won't allow you to give another plate now."

I sat with him on one plate. One of the havildars came and yelled, "Leave him, you eat first."

That hits me. I ate a little from his plate.

I went to bed at 7:30 p.m. Yes, it is another part of the Indian jail schedule. Everybody was sleeping, and I was the one who didn't sleep. I was thinking about my past life, how I spent all my life. My friends, girlfriend, and family... Suddenly, one thing clicked in my mind my friend is alive they will surely do my help. I will talk with them tomorrow. I got one ray of hope for tomorrow.

I was waiting for the morning.

"I wish I would have watched with me," I sighed to myself. A prisoner next to me heard what I said. He asked, "Do you want?"

"What?" I asked.

"Watch..." he whispered.

"do you have?" I asked.

"Yeah, I do." He showed his watch hiding from everyone. "It's great.." I yelled in an excited voice. "Shhh... Don't scream," he warned me. "you have to pay instead."

"What?" I asked.

"Money..."

"How much?" I asked.

"1000 rupees."

"What!" I shocked.

"It's okay if you don't want...!"

"No... no... I want it." I had some money in my bag and I only had 1000. I purchased that watch.

Now, it was only 9:00 pm, and I was waiting for tomorrow's 9:00 am; still, 12 hours were remaining. I was getting bored; I started playing with my watch. One of the havildars saw that I was still waking, so he scolded me, "307, sleep now..." I placed my watch under the pillow, and I slept. I got the arrangements for sleeping from Vinay, and he was the best guy. Vinay had promised me that he would also make some arrangements for the advocate. But, before him, there are also my friends who can help me out.

The darkest side of the jail was my night, with lots of dreams and overthinking. It was almost four or five days, but it seemed like it had been 4/5 months. Because there was no day and night I had felt in my jail.

My mind was only thinking about whether my family get to know or they would get the news but, they were not coming. I was at least expecting my brother and my mom to come here to release me from the Prison.

I didn't know what had happened. I was just waiting for them. I thought that there would be some compulsion. But is there any compulsion that bigger than me? My mind was running, just thinking of my family. My elder brother was smart and well-educated. At least he should try.

It was all my Imperfection that I had slipped for another girl.

Here is just my flame of eternal love, which converted into hate. I hated myself for loving a girl in this world. But, again, I have fallen for someone another, and she betrayed me just after I accepted her request. I thought about what I felt after she denied me so I didn't want anyone to behave like the same she did. That's why I respected her feelings and accepted her.

The surroundings were filled with "lack'ess, I could only see a lady coming to me. As far as she was coming, I could recognize her. She approached me and stood nearest to me in front. I wanted to call her but my voice was stuck in the trachea to say Aisha. I was feeling myself that I was not on the earth, but my feet were in the sky.

My body was on the earth, my spirit on the sky for her. I got up.

I didn't love Aisha Osman, she was only my friend. Why did she used to come in my dreams? 'It was a dream or reality. Or it's seriously, that my spirit leaves the body to meet her.' Questions were raised in my mind.

'Huh! Is this even possible? Soul and spirituality, all this is a big joke in the hearts and minds of people. And they firmly believe in all this.'

That dream did not feel like a dream.

I remembered Ayan's words when he said, "You never know the curse of the spiritual Heartache. And you hurt that spiritual heart." I started getting uneasy, grabbing my skull and sobbing.

Again the dawn started with the voice of the jailor constables, and everybody woke up. I got up and ran to go to the washroom. Because even if there is a slight delay, then the queue commences, and then the time is over. I know that I have been here for only three days, but I took the experience of this place in just 60 hours.

I went to the bathroom before all. The shower tap was very old. Lizards and cockroaches were already there everywhere in the bathroom. The spooky bathroom was decorated with webs. Anyhow I took a shower without standing in a queue. Suddenly, someone started banging on the bathroom door. I shouted, "Yes, I am coming out only."

Hurriedly, I wrapped a towel around my waist and moved out. One man stood in a row, he was staring continuously, "Look! Without me, no one can enter the bathroom. When I am done with my bath. Then you can all go." Pointing his index finger towards me. "Take care from next time or else I will naked you here by snatching the towel from your waist."

I nodded and went from there. Everybody was laughing at me...

The taste of prison and the taste of death is similar.

"Love is just strengthened nafs (satisfaction of evil mind)."

Expectations

Every hour I was waiting for my friend's response. I was not a criminal so every second was heavy on me. I saw my watch, it was showing 11:30 and it seemed since morning like it was the whole day.

Police staff came and announced lunch. While waiting for my friend's response, I did not feel hungry. Everyone was running for lunch but I stood there silently and was expecting that my friend would come. Vinay came and asked, "Brother, let's come for lunch."

"Hmm…" I nodded. He didn't force me and he went away. I sat on the corner of the prison where people came for the meeting.

I spent my whole day, neither his reply came nor he came.

'Maybe my expectations are so high. If it is not in my fate to be released from here, why I am thinking about it so much.'

It was 5:30 pm, my watch was waiting for him and I hadn't eaten anything since morning in waiting for him.

My brother like a friend left me at this stage. At least, I expected he would come.

"Always remember, there will be a time when no one will come to save you except God. No one came here for others, all are here for themselves. Humanity is not the human's priority now, not even now, but since the world started. The son of Adam killed his brother for the girl. These rituals have been going on since the world started. He didn't even see his brother for others, so do you think that is there anyone who will help you? Don't expect from the humans. And in this darkness, there's the only hope of God." Aisha's each word I was remembering.

Now, I started feeling hungry.

Vinay came and said politely as if he was an angel in all demons, "Come and eat, my family sent chivda for me. I don't borrow from anyone. You don't worry, I will serve you."

I woke up and went with him. I was walking with my loose legs, and I was feeling unconscious,

Aisha was looking toward me and she had a scythe in her hands. She was going to attack me and the one came and poured the water on me I opened my eyes and there were two police constables and Vinay were looking at me. All the prisoners were watching me as I was the first person who fainted.

Vinay gave me water, "you hadn't eaten since morning, maybe that's why you fainted." He brought his towel and wiped my face. He took me for the dinner. I ate dal rice and leafy vegetables.

I was still feeling weak. My legs were trembling.

With my trembling legs and the support of Vinay, I came back to my place.

I didn't have the strength to stand more. He helped me to sit on the floor.

I was watching the other prisoners were happy, and some of the others were sad.

It's a person's life, where people see positive and negative in the same thing.

Some people were happy because they got food for a living, and some people were sad because they were missing their families.

People whose vision was negative were the regretters and people whose vision was positive were ashamed people.

The reason I was there in the prison is the only I. Some of my biggest mistakes dragged me here.

My people were going far from me.

I was waiting for him till the next day. I was waiting for my family, friends, and any other advocates.

" The day will come when no one will be around you, except God. You have to deal it with yourself. When we are in our real homes in graves, people will be left us under 6 feet. They will continue their life, but you will be alone in the grave. You have to face the God's questions. He will be asked, what you did in the world when he sent you. At that time, you have to answer the questions which will be difficult for non-believers. Their tongue will be wanted to answer the questions but it won't be moved. So prepare for that day." _Aisha

I slept with the pain in my legs and pain in my heart. No one came for my bail.

The next day, I woke up at night before all the other prisoners. I was finding my watch and then I saw my watch was on 131 no. prisoner's hand. Gradually, I was trying to remove my watch from his hand. He woke up, and held my hand tightly he abused me and pushed me. I said, "This is my watch, I bought it."

Then he teased, "Okay! This is your watch, now take it with me" and he started playing with my watch, and all the prisoners woke up. They started cheering that prisoner. I was going to take my watch then he was taking it far from me.

At there, Vinay came and scolded him, "Return his watch." He weirdly saw me with his red eyes and threw on my face.

Vinay was going to slap him, but he saved himself and laughed at him. Vinay said, "Okay, let's go."

My under-eye was swollen after he threw it on my face.

I saw my watch, its glass had broken. I knew that time was bad, but the time on the same watch would come good.

I went for breakfast and I drank tea. Again, the same waiting for someone would come and take me out of there.

Now it had happened in only seven days which I had felt like 700 days. I was imprisoned for 7 years. I was scared just thinking about it.

What were days, what were nights, I wasn't understanding anything. Every day, the same things were going on, for 3000 days, but in reality, 30 days passed.

Gradually, I was also going to be a part of a prison.

Now, I felt this prison was home and prisoners as homies.

Life was going to be scary as days passed.

We had done our breakfast. At 9:15 a.m., one of the prisoners overran towards me and said, "One advocate come to meet our Daksh." I was surprised, and with my curiosity to meet him, I ran with my enthusiasm.

Police stopped me, and asked, "Where are you going?"

"My advocate came for my bail, let me go."

He shouted, "Which advocate? Is this the day of meeting the advocate? Go back from here."

"Don't trust anyone until you haven't analyzed him. Only trust in God, Indeed, he won't break your trust." _Aisha.

I was coming back disappointed. My tears filled my eyes, but it wasn't coming out.

Everybody was looking at me.

"From tomorrow, you will also do work over here. Do you know cutting wood?" said the constable staring at me when I was returning.

I replied, "No, sir."

"Then go and practice now onwards. You will also have to work."

I came with no words. He was laughing at me the one who lied to me. I went nearer to him and slapped him hard. He stopped laughing and started staring at me. When I was coming back after beating him, he came from behind and grabbed my neck with his hand. I hit his stomach with my elbow. He held his stomach for some seconds. Then he came back and pushed me so hard that I fell on the floor. I gathered my courage and got up to hit him and he pushed me hard by his foot.

I fell with such force that I placed my right elbow on the ground to save my head. And that elbow got injured and I started feeling dizzy. Everything seemed dark to me. Again I stood to beat him but he kicked me again and I fell to the ground. I started writhing in agony for some time and suddenly darkness started appearing in front of my eyes. I was unable to understand anything and became unconscious.

The jailor constables took me to the hospital. I was unconscious until we reached the hospital. I took my consciousness back, and I saw the doctors standing around me. When I completely woke up, they made me sit in the wheelchair and took me to the X-ray room.

They took an X-ray and I was waiting for the report. The X-ray technician declared, "he had fractured his right elbow. We have to admit him and he needs physical therapy."

They took me for physical therapy. They plastered my hand.

I felt like I should remove my hand from my body. Because it was giving me dreadful pain. They sealed my right hand. And sent me for the rest. Normally, I was afraid of being hospitalized. But, today I was happy to be hospitalized.

Things were complicated. I left my dream behind and moved on with the prisoner. I accepted myself as a sinner. And I was.

I made the biggest mistake in my life by accepting her love even after getting deceived.

Yes, she deceived me.

I am not saying that I am not sinful. I am the biggest sinner.

Now, my sin was having intercourse with her even after Aisha taught me about how to treat a woman.

I was lying on the bed and questions roamed in my mind, 'How to face this cruelty?' I closed my eyes, "If you hurt someone, what you think you will be live freely your life." Aisha was stood near my bed. I was frightened and got up. 'Fuck! It's a dream!' I murmured.

I rested on the bed after therapy. Anyhow I slept after a long time on a bed. It was cosy and comfortable. But the pain in my elbow didn't let me sleep at night. Anyhow I was attempting to sleep. The nurse came and gave me the pills for bedtime and less ache.

After some time I got shuteye.

Love is the story of time. If time ends the story, Love automatically ends.

Favor

★★★

"Freedom won't get you if you suicide. It is the biggest mistake that we humans commit in our temporary world. We left the world by committing suicides, but hereafter, till the resurrection we died frequently in the same manner as we died in suicide. Every time we commit suicide and die. We live again and commit suicide. This will have happened till the end of the world. God will give us this punishment."

"If suicide is not the solution. So what else is other? Do I get her again? Perhaps you don't know the meaning of love. You must have never loved anyone." I sighed.

"Every soul tastes the love in life.

You Know, Love is unexplainable, but it can be understood by experience.

Everybody has their own experience of their love story. For some it is fair and for some people it is poor. Because everybody is just creating their story on their own. They don't let their story on God. Only he can recuperate it. Because the Love story was written by God when we all were accumulated on the seventh sky it's named Rooh e Alamin. We accumulated over there before the world started. All the spirits of people who lived in the world were unaware of everybody. Have you ever wondered how one person loves unconditionally a person he met just before seconds, even if we met thousands of people in the world, why only we love that one person only?" Aisha was explaining to me and she asked one of the questions that made me wonder.

As the sun began to set, I and Aisha sat side by side on the beach, our toes buried in the sand. The waves crashed against the shore, creating a soothing rhythm.

"No, I haven't thought about it. Do you know?"

"Because when we were accumulated on Rooh-e-alamin (the seventh sky), that person whom you love was around you only. You and Krishna were together on Rooh-e-alamin. And there you both liked each other.

When God sent us down, he made us forget all the talks that were going on in the seventh sky. We were all promised by God that 'we would live in the world with devotion and love.

But, at that time we not only just fall in love with that person only. Also, other people were around us we loved them too.

Like, here in this temporary world, we meet temporary people and fall in love with them. Whether they are friends, girlfriends/boyfriends, relatives, etc.

Okay, I can understand that, we live with family so we are attached after living with them since childhood.

What about friends? We met at a time, loved each other, and brought affection. The reason is, that our spirits before entered the body had already met each other. Hence, when we met each other and started falling in love with that person."

I was hypnotized by her talking. I was watching in her eyes. Her almond-shaped eye was shining from incisions. I had only seen her eyes before. But while talking, she removed her niqab (nose piece). Her beauty was glowing not only from her look but also from her beautiful heart.

She was not very fair and not very dark. The colour of the skin was pale brown. Her beautiful dark brown eyes and almond shape were as attractive as the sun setting in the sky. Her nose was not much sharped and not much blunt. A normal-sized nose was not very attractive. The lips were beautifully designed. She was not only attractive from her face but also from her heart, mind, and more from her talks.

An Imaginary spotlight on her face by nature. Wherever she walked, she spotted.

Because I was also attracted without looking at her beauty. Just from her talks.

She was one of the gods gifted to her parents.

I couldn't define her age at that time. Maybe she was around 25-28 years old.

I was 23 years old at that time.

She asked, "Are you satisfied with my words?"

I replied, "Indeed, your words are valid. I am being attentive."

"So, don't ever try suicide in your life."

"I have one doubt, why we didn't recognize a person in the beginning but we have already met before."

"See, it is not allowed that we talk so deeply. But, you have a doubt, so I am telling you. God created us and we promised him that we only pray for him and always share love. But, human nature is differently designed by God. We can control our emotions a get but not love and feelings. Yes, we can control ourselves only when we learn to control ourselves for the sake of God."

"Can I know your religion?" I asked.

"Islam." She replied delicately.

"Okay!"

"Religions are the only names. God is only one. We changed their name to change worshipping manner according to our comfort. By the way, to whom do you worship?"

"I am an atheist. I don't believe in any God."

"I can understand that this age may take us on a different route. But, this is also the correct age to define our devotion present in the corner of our hearts. Idolization whomever you want to worship, but at least believe in God. In the eyes of God, humans who believe in other God are far better than those who don't believe in any God."

I was only listening to her. Her talking took so long that even the orange sky turned black. The sea reflected the stars. The whole sky was just filled with stars and one moon. The sky was more shining because of Mumbai's lights.

She hurried, "It's time to go." She got up and went to her house. She came like a fairy to save me as this is not normal in real life. Who cares about others? She didn't even know me, still, she saved me and also made me so strong so I couldn't take this step next time.

She taught me at once, that humanity still exists.

Her every word was meaningful for me to not attempt suicide next time.

"Bye!" I waved at her.

I went home with my thoughts.

It was just an hour with one stranger and I started thinking about her.

I reached my home. My whole spirit was there only. The emptiness I was feeling. I went out with depression, stress and anxiety. Then I came back with relief, peace and happiness on my face.

I saw myself in the mirror, my face had some glorious shine, with her talks and came back with a new life.

"Excuse me, it's time for your dinner. Go and get it for yourself." Breaking my thoughts one of the nurses came and commanded.

"But, it will be a difficult challenge for me to eat and take dinner with my own."

"So what do you want? You want me to feed you?"

I nodded and woke up and I stood in the queue. I took my dinner and I sat on my bed. I was going to eat my first bite, I remembered my friend Vinay, who always supported me. I wish I could feed him this food. Yeah, it was tasty.

Simple, Plain food was tasty for me in this prison world.

My memories with Aisha were bewildering. Whenever I missed her, I cried. I was the person who never cried before. I was a Playboy of my time. But, life had fun with me. Aisha is one of the outstanding girls with spirituality inside her. Her spirituality was taking me closer to her. 'Till now I had not loved her. But, I think I started loving her. I am passionate towards her.' Her words echo in my heart whenever a hard situation falls on me.

The nurse came and said, "Take your pills."

I took it from her and I ate it.

She offered me water.

I lay down on the bed, resting my back on the bed which was slightly leaned. She asked, "Is everything fine?"

"What type of question you are asking? I am not in my home." I said rudely.

"Yes, I know that. Why you have been arrested?" she said, sounding calm.

"Please Ma'am, leave me alone. Already I am worried." I sobbed. I was too worried that I didn't want to talk with anyone.

"Oh, Sorry sir. You are looking decent and belong to a good family that's why I asked."

She kept all the medicines on the table which was on my right side.

"I thought, you need some pity. Sorry. Do some rest."

I realized that I shouldn't behave like this. So I called her, "Nurse!"

She was going back to her work, When I called out, she looked back and said, "Yes, anything needs you?"

"Yes, Indeed! I need you."

She chuckled, "Are you flirting with me?"

I laughed, "No! Of course not! By the way, Myself, Daksh. You?"

"I am Aisha."

I kept silent.

"What happened?" She broke the silence.

"No, no... Alright! I am feeling sleepy."

"Do rest now! Sleep peacefully!" She started leaving.

"Bye! Bye!" I smiled.

"Bye, Good Night Daksh. So sweet name." She grinned.

I saw her going and laughed at myself.

'How fool I am. I just heard her name and I felt silent. Am I attracted towards her? Or am I just indebted to her for her favours?'

Questions were raised in my mind, She had done nothing less for me. She did everything for me whenever I needed it.

'If all those things she used to do for me is love, then the love I did with Krishna, what was that?'

I closed my eyes, trying to forget everything and sleep peacefully.

'If we love them we also have to repay it.'

_Hamza Khan.

Sins

"Good Morning Daksh!" The nurse came with morning medicines.

"Have you done with your breakfast?"

"Done," I replied.

"Sir, take your pills." She said softly.

I ate all the medicines that she gave me.

"Is it paining?"

I shook my head, "Yes! It is!"

"It will be fine soon and soon you will be at your home."

Her words were a blessing. She was a good nurse.

Who knew how for to care their patients, to treat their patients well.

Her smile heals every patient. Maybe all the patients were healed by her only. She was going back for her work and I sought her name, "Aisha,"

She turned, and chuckled, "You took my name?"

"No one called you by your name?"

She grinned, "what can I help you?"

"Are you free now, I want to talk."

"No I am busy right now, but it's okay, we will talk. Because you are so handsome and charming." She admired.

I laughed, "Thank you, Aisha."

"What's your full name? Where did you live?" I asked casually.

"Aisha Afzal Shaikh, I belong to Thane. But my native is Ramgarh. And I love to work here in my native place."

"Miss Shaikh." I arched one eyebrow.

She corrected, "Mrs. Shaikh."

"Oh, you are married?"

"Yeah." She smiled and she went from there. "It's okay, I have some work, I will see you later, bye!" she waved at me and went for her work.

'And She was Aisha Osman Khan.' My tears were flowing from the side of my eyes.

I ran towards the beach where I met her. I was finding her here and there and everywhere. I found her in the cloudy weather at the end of June when I didn't have any idea when the rain would happen. I didn't have an umbrella or raincoat. There was no roof I around so that I could go under it for my protection. The rain started falling, every person was running to save themselves. Someone had their umbrella or Raincoat.

Rain was heavily occurring. For two days there was no rain in Mumbai. So, the umbrella and raincoat were not with me. I was drenched. I had one watch I oftentimes brought with me without any occasion. My obsession with watches is different from another.

Afternoon, correct noon there was darkness in the sky like darkness arose in my life. Thick drops were dropping on my face and body. My hair got damp. I set my hair back from both hands, thinking of her. I was finding her in the smog of rain. Rain was heavily occurring. All the water was not logging but that whole water came down by slope and absorbed in the sands of the beach.

The dark cloudy weather was looking really beautiful. The peace in the rain and the support of a negative mind in dark weather, I got those both at once. I sat down on the footpath for one hour.

I started sneezing two to three times at once. The cold caught me.

I got a café near me. I bought a cup of coffee from there. I drank the coffee without blowing it. Warmness came into my body and I felt well.

The rain slowed down a bit. I went outside to find her again. I walked to the Bandra station. My leg was paining, It was raining drizzling. 'What if I had taken her phone number? I forgot man, fuck!' and I kicked on the big stone.

"Oh shit, it's hurting," I screamed in pain.

I was not doing these in love, but the affection raised in my mind for her. The real supporter I was feeling when I met the first time. I thought she could only help me to heal my heart. After Krishna's incident, I didn't trust in love. She ditched me and stabbed me in my back. How did I come back from the point of committing suicide? Because of that woman. I had no desire to live again. But she gave a ray of life. I was indebted to her.

I took a taxi and I went back to my home. My knee was paining. I was being stubborn even though I had not thought about myself and my family.

My family had already been upset with me.

They didn't like me. I reached my home. Father saw me and he made faces. I thought mom would support me but she just supported her husband.

I went inside my room and I shut the door. I heard my father's voice, "See your son, your son is prospering rude day by day. I forgave him for what had he done with us. He does a sin, not the mistake.

This does not mean that he should repeat the sin. He had kept the girl with him on the pretext of studying. "

My mom began too, "Every time I have to listen to his father's scolding because of him."

I opened the bathroom door, my elder brother opened it simultaneously. I shouted, "Get outside brother."

"It's okay my little brother, chill." He replied pleasantly and he moved outside. He was the only one in my family who supported me on every path. If the path was not right, so he denied me by doing that thing.

I changed my clothes and lay down on the bed. 'I wish I could meet her.'

My brother entered back in the room. And saw my drenched hairs which were wet by rain when I was outside.

He threw the towel and I caught it.

"What the hell bro, why are you beating me with a towel."

"Dry your hair." He commanded, angrily.

I took a towel and I dried my hair.

"Everything alright?" He asked softly.

"Of course brother, but now, let me sleep."

"Yeah, I have to do my work outside. You Sleep. And don't lock the door from inside."

"Ok, boss!" I said lying on the bed.

I was going to stop him to off the lights of the room.

Before I said, he off the lights and went outside.

"Daksh! Daksh!" She was waking me up by patting me on the back.

"Yes! Everything alright?" I asked, opening my sleepy eyes.

"Daksh, how do you do?" Nurse Aisha asked in a musical tone.

"Aisha?" I confusedly asked. "Aa…I am good." I grinned.

"You look too cute when you are smiling. I wish you always smile like this, Amen." She turned both her praying hands over her face.

"Thank you!"

She said, "Now stand up and come with me for dressing. It's time to dress your bandage."

"Sure, I'm coming," I replied.

She told me to sit. The doctor came and asked while pressing my hand, "Is it paining?"

"Yes, doctor."

"Okay, I will dress it first."

The Doctors were really good there. I thought doctors would be ill-mannered in the municipality hospital, but they were indeed good.

They dealt with me well. I saw nurse Aisha she was helping doctors when they were treating me. When I was suffering from pain, she was also feeling pain. I was writhing in pain and she was looking at me. My pain in hand was not much paining than my heart. In this tragedy, I got all the truth about my friends and love. Both these pains were becoming a burden on me. I couldn't bear it.

Then I remembered the words of Aisha,

'A good person's life is arduous, it is God's Choice who should be close to him. Chose persons by God are in difficult situations so that person prays to him.

God loves, it is as if his creation asked him something by core. So he loves to watch that person. Indeed, God doesn't burden upon any soul except to the extent of its strength.'

Life was not that much complicated.

Pleasing and beautiful scene I imagined in my thoughts. I took a deep breath in and then out. It was hard to forget Krishna, but my brain reminded my heart. I had lavished all my love on her. There was only one easy way to forget, and that was suicide.

Suicide, I had this option if I hadn't promised to someone.

I didn't believe in promises, but this time I did respect her and didn't want to break the promise.

It had been three days after I was admitted to the hospital. They told us to rest for seven days and I was wishing for four days either I should pass away or I should be released.

But there were still some consequences in my life that I had created. There were things that I did. If she had known about that day she would never have forgiven me and I would the life imprisonment.

'Should I clear all the things to Diya about that day? I am doing good at hiding Sanchit's mistake. If I did that, what if she again did a case on me? The trust already has been broken. No, I cannot take a chance to tell her. Or else I will be trapped more in this case.' I was getting worried about thinking.

But it all happened suddenly.

'Even one sin can make you the resident of hell, and that one deed can give you the best place in heaven.'

Like this,

'No matter how hard you try to win love, that one mistake can make you a cheater. Even if you cheat a million, if you say two or three loving words, you will become the key to that person's happiness. '

_Hamza Khan.

Heavy Burdens

"Heavy burdens are only words in this temporary world where people accept it as they cannot face it before they face it. Even if some people are not drowning, they show as if they are drowning. Do you understand what I wanted to say?" Nurse Aisha said.

She saw me I was crying. She asked me but I didn't reply. So she started talking to me and then she said this familiar sentence.

"I heard it somewhere else, the same," I said while thinking.

"What!" She chuckled.

"Yeah, you talked like Aisha."

She started laughing, "What are you saying?"

"Yes, you tell the same words which already said by Aisha. Her words and her thoughts have been roaming in my mind I was once I was imprisoned. I don't know, why?"

She stopped laughing.

"Wait Daksh, are you talking about Aisha." And she asked again for correction, "Aisha Osman?"

"Yes, but how do you know this? You recognize her name exactly. Even, I had forgotten her full name."

"Please don't say you are the same Daksh before eight months..."

I interfered, "What are you saying? Please clear it to me." First, she paused for some time. As the heavy burden falls on her.

First, he started thinking about something. Then, she stood suddenly from the chair. She was going to faint but she stabled herself by holding my hand. When she realized that I was holding her hand, Slowly released the handheld in my fingers and Teardrops started falling.

And then she started crying. First, she was cursing herself.

"What happened Aisha? What's going on? Are you alright?"

"Get lost from here. I never even knew you from now here. You destroyed everything about her for some months. You destroyed her. I am her best friend. How I saw her, I know well." She exclaimed.

"You are Aisha's best friend. That Aisha Osman?" I was shocked.

She started crying.

"Where is she now? Tell her I want to meet." I kept my wish.

"She was admitted to the hospital. Her condition is not good. What are you getting by destroying her? The curse of the spiritual Heartache." She shouted.

Doctors came hurriedly. She realized that she was in the hospital so she stopped crying. She wiped her tears from the tissue paper kept in the Apron.

Doctors didn't ask anything from her, as they were aware that was her issue.

She was the only person in the hospital who was caring for me a lot and she also left me.

'Now it has become a habit to be separated from people. Every attached person is leaving me. Has anyone asked about my heart? What does my heart want, what does it think, and for whom and why does it beat? I am saddest of all among the people of the whole world.'

"Daksh! When you are in trouble so ask God to help. And if you are cursing yourself because of the problems in your life, Always remember that God tests His loved ones. That is why his beloved servant should be engaged in worshipping him. Mankind is like that, if he is blessed without doing anything, he does not thank the one above. He thinks all it's getting because of himself. But he is unaware that‹ The giver of sustenance and the one who takes away sustenance are the same, the God. God tests them to realize this." Said Aisha Osman. I was getting all her meaning which she said to me once.

Suddenly, I caught a cold. I was feeling cold so I took my blanket on my body and I slept until noon. My eyes opened in the evening and I saw another nurse was reading the book. She was a bit old and a bit fat.

I asked her, "Where is Nurse Aisha?"

"She went to leave for some days." She replied and continued with her work.

'I am the reason for her leave.'

My eyes were addicted to crying and tears were wanted to come out. My heart was always frightened. And I saw Diya in front of me. "My eyes are deceiving me Like my life is biting the dust in my eyes," I grumbled to myself.

She listened and said, "I am Sorry Daksh."

I could not believe my eyes and ears.

I said, "What had to happen happened."

"I am taking my words back. Please forgive me." She was pleading.

"Are you in senses? It's my habit to live alone. Don't ask for forgiveness. Even I am sorry."

"Why are you sorry?"

"Diya." I paused and started thinking 'Should I tell her or not?'

"What Daksh?" she asked in a beautiful tone.

"Diya, now I am going to tell you about Sanchit."

"Before the day of the marriage function, I saw him talking outside with her girlfriend. She came with us because it was my friend's plan. I was forced into marriage, I didn't want to come into marriage. This was his plan and the married man would run away with his love. And we were with him. "

"What? What more you are hiding? I will include this in your case. I am going to tell this to the officer."

"I knew it. That's why I told you without any hesitation."

And that old and fat nurse shouted, "Daksh!" And I woke up and I was finding Diya around us.

I asked, "Do you see that girl sitting over here."

"Including me and that nurse, there is no other girl in this male ward. Maybe You were dreaming."

She gave me pills before dinner and I ate them.

"After 10 minutes, go and bring your dinner." She commanded.

'I knew that she would have behaved like she did in my dream. No, I cannot say her. I will let this be my secret. But, I have to say to her before my other friends speak. They do not know one thing and that is what had happened inside his room. If I spoke to Diya then I would only be trapped.

Do I tell her or not?' Questions were roaming in my mind, and the heart replied, "Tell her everything."

My brain was not ready to tell her about that incident.

And I heard it, Always listen to your brain if you have options between heart and brain. The brain is practical while on the other hand, the heart is emotional.

I listened only to my heart and now this time I would like to choose an option in my brain.

Relatives and family of every patient were going to have dinner. I went with my two legs and one hand. My other hand was of no use. I took a plate and dinner in it. Carefully I handled it and sat on my bed. I ate it and I found that there was not a single drop of water in my bottle. I woke up again walked to the water cooler and filled it with one hand. These works were a great challenge for me.

I ate my dinner and two constables were looking at me suspiciously. They thought that I would elope from here. How can I explain to them that I cannot do such things?

I was an innocent fool, would I be able to fool others? I should have to sleep but I was failing to sleep. I was travelling in a local train at 23:23. People were silent as they weren't on working hours.

Some of the people have jobs at night or somebody late at night. There was not much rush, I was feeling myself in the window seat. Stations are coming in 2 to 3 minutes. Some are boarding and some are descending. But, I don't care about them. I am enjoying my company in a train, running too fast from the wind, and by crossing trees, mountains, and cities it is also crossing the wind coming in opposite direction. I don't understand moon wants me or if I want the moon because I feel better about seeing the moon. That's the beautiful journey I was imagining and it always made me a smile on my face. Because I loved to travel at night on the train, especially on the Local Train.

It was my daily routine that I felt better first then I slept. It was also the one Aisha said to me.

She used to say,

'The day felt better, now create your night more cozy than that.'

Intensions

★★★

Intensely I want back her in my life to talk to, be friends with, and be a good partner to spend time with without stress and depression.

Street lights were on, I was walking on the footpath. I got one cane and started playing with it.

I kicked hard with my foot it goes and hit a woman she came to me, I was frightened and said, "Sorry ma'am!"

"Sorry? My foot! Can't tolerate seeing a girl going to her house at late night. People like you come to tease."

"Look ma'am, I am not flirting and not doing any kind of mischievous. I was just walking in my own miserable life. Sorry Ma'am."

"What sorry, You will do it yourself and then apologize? Let me call the police. Or 103."

"Please Ma'am, leave me I won't do it again."

"It means you are accepting that you did mischievous."

"No, I don't mean that."

She wasn't convinced and she called the police. I was going to escape from there but the Police came from my opposite direction and caught me.

They put me in their jeep where some other people were resting in a jeep.

One of the heavy drunks and he might be driving while drinking. And another one was caught while playing cards on the footpath. And I, the innocent was stuck between these people. We reached to the police station.

They were dragging me to put me in the lock-up.

"Sir! Sir! Sorry sir I was not doing intentionally." I begged. "Leave me, sir. Don't call my dad. Please, sir!"

I was explaining to him that I wasn't wrong. But they were not taking it on the ear.

It was my first time in lock up. I was surrounded by some goons in lock up. They were threatening me. "Officer! Officer! Look what are they doing! They are going to beat me." I yelled.

He scolded them and they got silent.

They called my dad after some hours in the police station.

My dad came and it was a night when nobody was coming for my bail. My father came and gave me a tight slap on my left cheek. I kept my hand on the left cheek. I swallowed hard.

He said softly, "Rot and die here. I won't come for your bail."

I was crying, "Dad please, don't leave me here. Dad, I was not doing anything. She was lying, dad." I started crying bitterly.

The inspector put me in the lock-up again.

I sat on the floor, some people were staring at me. I ignored them and closed my eyes. My intentions were good, but they didn't understand.

Mosquitoes were disturbing my sleep. I was killing mosquitoes one by one who sat on my body.

My whole sleepless night was passed by killing mosquitoes. I was stretching my t-shirt from my teeth and knees. My dad came and saw me doing this shit in the jail. I was shocked, "Dad!"

He came with one advocate. He told me to do a signature on bail papers. I signed wherever he said for signature.

I hugged my dad and said, "Love you too Dad!" when he didn't even say I love you to me.

He was still angry.

"Don't molest any girl. We should respect every woman."

"Dad, I was neither molesting her nor teasing her."

"Don't give me excuses Daksh, let's go home. Your mother was not tired of crying for you."

Now I understand that my father got me released because of my mother.

I was thinking that he loved me by heart and not showing his love for me. But, he had only hatred for me. I sat back in his car and he drove to our home. All the way, I was peeping out from the window. I was enjoying the song of Atif Aslam. He was my favourite artist compared to other singers.

His beats gave me the best heartbe"t. That beat controlled my heartbeat. My father was rapidly driving the car. And I saw Aisha at the corner of the beach. I said, "Dad stopped the car."

"What happened?" He asked repeatedly.

And he finally stopped his car and we were too far.

"Dad, Take a U-turn," I ordered.

"What happened? First, clear me that."

"Dad, there is Aisha."

"Who is she?"

"She is my…" I paused because I didn't know who was for me. Then I continued, "Friend! Yes, she is my friend."

"Again Girl." He said irritably.

He took a U-turn and she got me and I sought her name, "Aisha!"

She didn't move back. Again I shouted her name, "Aisha, it's me, Daksh."

She didn't turn.

I ran towards her and when I looked in front she was someone else.

But, her way of hijab was the same as Aisha wore.

I was confused and said to Dad, "No one is here, let's go home."

"Only knows how to do time pass." He murmured to himself and sat in the car.

I reached my home and my mom hugged me and started crying.

I didn't care about anyone, but used to think only about myself.

I went to my room and removed all my clothes through them on the bed.

I entered the bathroom first I took a shower then I slept in the bathtub with warm water. I was inside the bathtub for half an hour.

My eyes opened and my neck started giving severe pain. I was trying to fit my neck with my hands. The towel was hung inside the bathroom, I wrapped it around my waist.

I entered the bedroom while my brother was lying on the bed and asked, "Feeling relaxed?"

"It's feeling better now. I was tired the whole night lock-up." I replied.

"Don't worry, now you are alright." He grinned.

"You know, she falsely accused me." I kept my points.

"I know Daksh, I can understand. Here, take your new clothes. You have come out of lock-up, so a present for you."

I grinned and accepted his gift.

"Go and wear it." He demanded.

It was a white colour hoodie and dark blue cargo pants. I was fitted in that garments.

He stood and held my both shoulders tightly and said, "Don't leave us like that. We deteriorated in just one night without you. First, you left us for that Girl, and living with her is not the right way to live with a girl. If you love her then marry her. See, she left you because you didn't have a secure relationship." And he hugged me, "Please, be understandable." He grinned.

And I realized that 'there is at least a person who cares for me and he does have respect for me.'

I didn't say anything in reply and went outside. I was thinking about her and only her. 'Where would be she? Where would I get her?' like different questions were going in my head.

I had been looking for her for four days and still, I was searching for her. My days were spent on the streets one night was also spent in Lock Up.

Why I was so desperate to meet her I didn't know. Of course, she helped me, but I had never repaid for the favour.

'I want to meet her, to thank her, to talk to her, to know her. But, at least for once if she will meet, I will thank her.'

I thought she might have left the city. Without giving up hope, I continued to search for her.

Every time she spoke my heart got peace.

I had only one meeting with her even then my heart captured her. It might be because she saved my life. I went to the beach that day. The beach was fully rushed. And I was getting bored on that fully rushed beach. I was going out of that place meanwhile I saw one horse running and one woman sitting on the horse and riding a horse on the beach. Her horse was running too fast and she was carefully handling her horse.

I saw her from afar where the sun was drowning and she was riding a horse.

Her horse was running faster than every time.

She pulled on the rein, The horse raised both its front legs and turned away. She stopped the horse and jumped from the horse. She paid money to the horse owner and everybody around her was clapping. I was also clapped for her. I was a little bit far from her.

When I looked at that woman carefully, she was Aisha. I ran towards her and I yelled, "Aishaa…."

I exclaimed, "You finally got me."

She stared suspiciously, "you were finding me?" pointed her finger towards herself.

"Sorry, I was being over-excited."

"No, it's okay you can express your excitement. But, why do you find me?"

"I started feeling a desire to meet you in my heart. Once I met you, I became such a firm friend." I replied.

She looked at me and grinned. She looked more beautiful than I saw her the first time. As I already said, the glow-up naturally came to her face. The spotlight was spotted only on Aisha. Spotlight by nature. For the first time, my intention was so pure to one girl.

'No matter how you have grieved in your life, All the griefs bow down in front of that one happiness.'

_Hamza Khan.

July Evening

July evening, I met her finally. I needed her the most at this time. The time when everyone was leaving me alone. I didn't have a friend. I had those but they were in Delhi and some other place.

Rain was slowly precipitating and drop by drop we were drenching. She offered her umbrella, "Here, come in my umbrella."

I grabbed this friendship's first offer. I asked, "Friends?" I came out of the umbrella and came in front of her extending my hand of friendship towards her.

She didn't reply.

"Aisha, be my friend. I don't have any of the friends in my life right now. I have been feeling lonely since Krishna left me. I had one option in my life but you saved me from that option." I mumbled.

"I can understand, what happens when you are alone in the whole world." She consoled.

"She was the only one whom I used to love more than anyone else in the world. I loved her so much that no one has ever loved. I have made many sacrifices for her. Still, she deceived me." I sighed.

"Are you assuring that you loved her so much more than anyone then listen. You are saying that you sacrifice? Do you know Adam?" She asked.

"Yes, the first person on this earth," I replied.

"I am going to narrate his love story. Can I?" She asked.

The rain had stopped. Sky coloured with pink itself. Birds in the sky were going back to their home. She sat down on the wet bench and I sat next to her. Carefully, I was listening to her narrations.

"God created Adam. When Adam was feeling lonely in Paradise, God created a woman from the bent rib of man. God created your woman with your bent rib, and that woman in your fate will come in contact with you, and your heart will be beat because your one part is with your soulmate. Okay! Let's continue, When Adam saw her, he fell for her.

Adam started loving her and she also loved him too. They spent many times together in heaven.

One day they were provoked by Satan and God expelled them from heaven. The story is not till here.

God punished them. Adam and Eve were put on separate sides of the earth. Adam and Eve searched for each other for forty years on the earth. Where there was no existence except them.

They were not tired of searching for each other. Adam loves Eve unconditionally. And Eve loves Adam unconditionally.

They found each other after forty years.

It was that era where nobody lived on earth except animals. He did not give up and finally found her. This is Love.

It doesn't happen that every person comes and shouts I love you.

We have to fulfil and also have to give tests in love." She recalled the wonderful story about Love.

"It's the most wonderful story I ever heard."

I appreciated her storytelling.

"I will explain to you the meaning of love every time then only resolve that the girl you are watching is attraction, affection, or love." She explained.

I caressed my wet hair and said, "Sure."

She said, "Let's go home. I am offering you a hot coffee in my house."

"This is your second offer of friendship. But not today." I gushed.

"Yes, you are my good friend now. With this new relationship of friendship, I will give you a treat tomorrow." She declared.

"I have to leave now! I am so glad to meet you again." I said, gladly.

"We will often meet with each other." She laughed softly.

"Remember! My friendship is not in everyone's fate, so be careful." She chuckled.

"I will not let this friendship break, I promise." I kept my promise by taking her talks seriously.

"I was kidding, Daksh." She chuckled.

"If I wanted to meet you again, so what should I have to do?" I asked.

"Here, take my phone number, this is my favourite place I oftentimes come here to ride a horse and watch the sunset, I love this." She said her choices, excitedly.

"Then it's dining, we will meet here tomorrow if you can," I asked.

"Of course, I only have offered you to come to my house for a coffee or a dinner." She said.

"Oh Sorry! I forgot." I bite my tongue between my teeth.

"We will meet tomorrow, Bye!" she waved at me.

I shook my head, "Bye!"

'What an amazing woman she is! She rides horse so fast and she is an expert in everything.' I was walking back to my home. I caught a cab to go home and sleep peacefully. Which had not been completed for days.

The waiting of the next day was a different kind of excitement. My brother was sleeping beside me, I remembered the moment when she was kidding. When I memorized those moments I laughed a bit. My brother turned to me and asked, "Yes! What happened, why are you laughing alone."

"Nothing brother, I remembered one old joke." I lied.

"You liar! Tell me true!" he chuckled.

"Okay, do you want to laugh?" I asked.

" Yes!" he answered.

"Are you sure?" I asked again.

He closed his eyes and shook his head.

As soon as he said yes, I started tickling him. "Stop it, man!" He said while suppressing his laughter.

"I will not stop now!"

"It won't hold! Well, take this!" And he started tickling me too.

"Okay, okay. Let's just do it, brother." I said while holding back my laughter.

I placed my head on his chest and hugged him and fell asleep. My brother was slowly patting me on my back and making me sleep.

The next day, I woke up early in the morning. There was a sunny weather. I wear it according to the weather. A light blue colour shirt with dark blue colour pants.

I went out without breakfast. I sat on the beach before the time. I waited there for five hours at the beach. Watching people living their lives with their loved ones. Spouse, children and parents.

I glanced at my watch. It was 4:00 p.m. The sun was playing hide and seek. The weather was going to be more cloudy as time passed.

Suddenly, raining started. I was still sitting there waiting for her because her arrival time had come close. I was drenched. The beach behind me was passing the cold breezes. I was feeling cold. Then, the one cab arrived. Aisha was sitting in that cab. She came out of it and paid to the cab driver. Till I reached near her, she sent the cab back. She too didn't have the umbrella.

She was searching the roof for protection from the rain.

I ran near to her, and called her, "Aisha! Here I am!"

"Oh my God! You are wet."

"You too!" and we chuckled.

After five to ten minutes of finding rides we got one taxi, and we hired a taxi. Drenched we, sat in the car.

Taxi drivers were playing Old classic Bollywood songs. I enjoyed the song. I asked her taste in song, "Which kind of songs do you like?"

"I don't like songs and kinds of music." She said while focusing somewhere else.

"Really? I mean aren't you kidding?" I vaguely asked.

"Is this the time for kidding?" She replied.

Drops of rain were coming inside a taxi. We closed the windows of our respective seats. We enjoyed the July monsoon while travelling. The weather changed suddenly from sunny to rainy. The dark black weather where taxi driver needs to on their headlights.

"What are you doing, I mean which profession?"

"I am a teacher in Kindergarten school." She said, proudly.

"That's great!" I replied.

"Stop here in front of B wing." She commanded to taxi driver. We reached her apartment and descended from the taxi.

She paid money to the taxi driver. I saw her apartment it was the old 7-floor building in Mumbai. And she used to live on the 4th floor. We entered into her apartment. There was an old elevator. She opened the grills of the elevator, pressed the 4th floor button and the elevator stopped at the fourth floor. I pull the sliding grills of the elevator. She moved out finding her keys from her purse. She opened the door and entered her house. All around in the house were smelled of Sandalwood and rose.

I sat on her sofa. It was a bit old and the whole walls were coloured by light green colour. Flowers were decorated on the window. She entered in bedroom and found clothes for me. She came outside and said, "Go and dry yourself in the bedroom and change your clothes." She offered me a shirt and pants, "This is a new one but no one wore this shirt. Wear this until it won't be dried."

I asked, "Is this your father's shirt?"

"My father and my mother left me when I was born.

And uncle left me when I needed him the most.

And Aunty get free by giving me to the stranger"

"Who was that stranger?" I asked.

"Who knows stranger?" She replied. "Go and change now." I didn't know which bedroom she was talking about.

She moved inside the bedroom. I was sitting in the dining room. But realizing that her house getting mud because of me I entered the bedroom while unbuttoning my shirt. I was changing clothes meanwhile Aisha came out of the bathroom in her inner garments. I was stunned to see her.

I went closer to her and she was attracted to me too. She was so close that her lips were touching my chest and my heartbeat was feeling her lips. I only buttoned my upper collar. My whole body was appearing. Her black tight bra wasn't more attractive than her wet-tied hair. My lips were going to kiss her hair. And I realized that she would be afraid of me. And I moved back. I didn't try any of my moves that hurt her.

I apologized, "Sorry." Meanwhile, I was saying, she was embarrassed, "I forgot to say which bedroom you should go to." I opened the bedroom door and came outside. And heaved a sigh of relief.

After some time I heard a voice of her crying.

I slightly opened the door and I saw her. She was in prostration and was crying pleadingly.

"God, forgive me. I was going to take a big step towards the sin. I was going to impure my soul. God, what do I do now? I am the biggest sinner in the world, God you are merciful, You are the God of the whole world. God bless some mercy on me."

I was regretting about what I did. And also I was thankful to God that I stopped before taking another step. She was so pure that I couldn't even think of having sex with her. She was the first girl when I went to her bedroom but was allowed myself out without doing anything.

She came after one hour and said, "Sorry, I forgot to make coffee."

"You were crying?" I asked.

"No, I was regretting, I remembered my past sins, and asked forgiveness from God."

"You are such a spiritual girl, who doesn't need to ask forgiveness. You don't even touch the sins, so why apologize?" I raised a question.

"We don't know what sin we committed unknowingly, whose heart got hurt. So, if we ask forgiveness to God, he forgives us."

"But, if I would ask forgiveness he wouldn't forgive me," I said.

"God loves those who return to Him. Apologizes to him." She replied.

"I apologized again." Rolled down my eyes.

"You don't need to worry." She said, "Okay, I will bring a coffee for you."

We went to the balcony which was decorated with flowers, and a tiny garden. Beautiful flowers were planted on the balcony, and the smell of the sand was giving therapy to me.

An extended roof on the balcony which protected us from rain, we were drinking coffee stood inside it.

There was a small tea table, I kept my cup on it.

"May I leave now?" I asked permission.

"Okay, now you know my home if you need me don't find me here and there." She chuckled.

"Thank Aisha for the Coffee." I laughed.

"Next time again, sure." She grinned.

After so many embarrassing moments I created, she still talked to me.

'The fascinating tale of love is that if it is true, so it only cares about her.'

Krishna (Daksh Past)

'Krishna was my childhood friend. She has been my friend since the time my mother used to drag me to school. I was used to creeping outside the school, my mom used to scold me in front of everyone.

Monday morning, it was raining. Mom was trying to make me wear gumboots. I drove to the school with much frenzy.

When I entered the classroom with tears in my eyes. One girl offered me her handkerchief to wipe my tears.

I took it from her and threw her hankie on the floor. She picked me up and said, "It's okay if you don't want to. But, don't cry" She was persuading me.

I stopped crying and we sat on one bench. From that day to till 10th standard we had never separated. We were the best buddy and the best friend.

I had feelings for her and she also had feelings for me too.

And finally, I talked when I was in 10th class, "I Love You, Krishna."

She accepted and replied to my magical words, "I love you too." She hugged me and I hugged her too.

Now, we were a couple. We oftentimes lived with each other.

The next day result is displayed. I also got the low marks and she got the highest marks above distinction.

Her dad decided to take her admission to St. Xavier's College Mumbai and I didn't get that high ratio so I could also be admitted there. I got admission, it was a normal college in Mumbai. Our meetings gradually decreased.

It was the time when I was used to be a Playboy so I don't have that one only. Also, I had two girlfriends whom I was dating.

And I was easily trapped by the girls in my love life. I wasn't in love with them but the one Krishna was attached to the core of my heart and I, the person like Daksh who never falls into this rubbish fell for Krishna after some time. In the beginning, she was not much more for me but as time passed she made her palace in my heart.

Her heartbeats were crossover with my heartbeat.

When her heartbeats stopped I was not sufficient for living.

The day when I and she wasn't talking on phone calls, days passed as I hadn't eaten food that day. With the emptiness in my life, I passed my days without her. It is not that if we fight then the conversation stops. When her father was at home she was not allowed me to talk to her.

I had broken up with all my girlfriends and stopped talking with my female friends. It was the huge sacrifice of my life.

When everything I denied from my life then I had only Krishna.

I loved her from my heart that I didn't tell her. We were talking to each other and she wasn't interested in me. She considered that I don't Love her and I am pretending to love her.

The day she told me when I called her, "Look Daksh, I know you are a playboy and you are pretending that you are loving me. Please, stop this showing off."

I replied to her, "No, Absolutely no Krishna. I love you and I want you forever in my life." I said in my quavering voice.

She neglected everything I spoke to her.

When I didn't Love her and she was begging me I denied her every word. I was only pretending that I was listening but my whole mind is diverted somewhere else.

The day she told me about her feelings of reflection my eyes were looking figure of her body when we were in 12th class. I said, "It's okay darling. Come on let's enjoy." And her waist was visible when her crop t-shirt slightly moved up. I touched her waist with my three fingers and gradually I hold her waist with both hands. I picked her up and put her in my car. I closed the car's door and started kissing her.

I was brutally kissing her, she was exhausting. I was removing my T-shirt when only I got a call from my dad, "Where are you?"

"I came to my friend's abode, I will be back in half an hour."

"Come urgently." He shouted.

I said irritated, "Let's meet tomorrow, dad is calling me.

"I was enjoying dude." She said.

" I have to go, otherwise, I would have left her only after the program." I came out and wore a T-shirt. I told her to wear her T-shirt and I sat in the driver's seat. I took a car from there and dropped her house.

I reached my house.

My father asked loudly, "Tell me the truth where were you? Where is my car?"

"I was at my friend's home Dad. I took your car and I took it back right now, you may see it."

"Don't lie to me."

"So, what do you think where I was?"

He said by gazing down, shamefully, "I saw you at our corner street you were shirtless outside your car, I saw a girl with you."

I was afraid. I said, "No Dad, that was not me. You can call my friend he will answer you."

I dialled his number and he picked up, "Hey buddy, how was the night with your girlfriend." My friend asked excitedly.

"Look, I listened," Dad said. "I got my answer."

"Hello! Hello!" My friend pretended, and he cut the call.

"What should I tell now?" He said slowly.

Then he suddenly shouted, "What should I say?"

"Sorry, Dad." I apologized.

"Get out of here. Get out?" And since that day, I have fallen from my parent's grace. They don't believe in me. And that was my life's first lesson that I did wrong.

But, I started loving her. After some months I decided to tell her everything. And I went to her and expressed everything she hadn't accepted.

I was yearning for her love. I have undergone many hardships to get her.

I became so determined to achieve her love, to achieve her.

My graduation was going to be completed. My whole college life was destroyed because of loving her.

The day, where she came to me and accepted me to live with her. But she had a condition.

"What condition Krishna? Our relationships will now be built on these bonds. On condition?" I asked.

"Look dear, if we tell our parents they refuse us. They won't be ready for our marriage. You haven't even got ready for your future. Are you getting?" she asked.

I nodded. Then she continued, "So be ready, we will start living in a live-in relationship in Delhi. Make whatever excuses at your home."

I had completed my graduation. I asked my father for a master's outside Mumbai.

In the beginning, he was not allowing me to go outside of Mumbai.

Then I became an obedient child in front of their eyes. They knew that he would do something wrong in his life still they allowed me to go outside. I got admitted to Delhi.

I got the chance to get into a live-in relationship. We went to New Delhi on the last flight. She lied in her house and she got a job in New Delhi. Their parents were not allowing her to move out. But she was emotionally asked by their parents and they accepted. She lied that her transfer had been done to New Delhi. If she left this job then she wouldn't get this job again. She joined a job in New Delhi.

She was sending money to her parents every month only 5000 rupees and she got 35,000 from her job. The rest of the money she saved for our marriage. Not only her contribute to saving money but also I contributed my pocket money for marriage.

I attended my college daily from 10:00 to 5:00 pm. Krishna was attending her job from 9:00 am to 5:00 pm.

Every night we made it so beautiful. I was on the bed with her. Spent the night gorgeously with her.

Our lives were going too smoothly. I got my friends there, Sanchit, Ananya, Vivek, Ayan, Pranjal, Shiva and Manasi.

Every Sunday evening Krishna kept a dinner party for my friends. Our lives were too easy without any burdens.

One day I went to Mumbai and she lived there again because of work. I forced her to come with me but she declined. So, I leave her alone in New Delhi.

I said, "I will be back in 3 days."

She said, "Please come soon. I will miss you."

"Yeah baby, I will. Take care" I kissed her forehead. I moved out and wiped my tears for her. The live-in relationship was about to be completed one year in five days. When I reached the airport, I got the news that there was no flight due to bad weather conditions in Mumbai. So I returned after wasting 7 hours at the airport and travelling to my house. I thought that I would go to Mumbai by the morning train tomorrow. So, I returned to my house. I was about to ring the doorbell but I thought she would be disturbed so I removed the keys to my home from my bag. I opened the door. I got that the lights were on in the bedroom. I grinned and started thinking, 'She is too hardworking girl.' And I was about to surprise her when she gave me a surprise with a man in our room. I asked worried, "Who is he? What he is doing right now?"

She explained, "Don't worry, he is my colleague. Helping

Me to complete my project. I have to give this tomorrow."

I was going to ask something she said, "Thank God you came. Now you will also be here with us." When she said this I got relieved. I slept in my bedroom and they were working in the living room. Suddenly my eyes opened at night and when I went to check them, I saw that both of them were working. I breathed a sigh of relief and went back to sleep. The next day, I found Krishna next to me and her colleague was sleeping in the living room.

They both went to their work and I came for my vacation of two days. When I came to Mumbai, I called her.

She said, "Oh, I was going to call you."

"It's not a coincidence, it's your heartbeats that I listened from here."

"Stop this rubbish. Thanks for supporting me till here. Now I am going abroad with Kabir. Kabir was the one who was my colleague that night." She said shamelessly and declined the call.

I called her back, "What kind of kidding you are doing Krishna? Don't give me such a heart attack."

"I am not kidding. When I came to Delhi, I realized why should I spend my life with a stray boy when a boy like Kabir was following me, loving me and most importantly Caring for me. Now don't call me. Goodbye."

'I was taking care of you too. I loved you very much too. I had also improved to some extent. Why did you leave me?' I screamed and shouted. Nobody heard me.

I was there at the corner of Marine lines and when I tried to go in front of the vehicle you saved me. And I got another life to live.'

I narrated.

Aisha didn't reply. She felt silent and she started thinking and said, "I am making dinner. Eat before you leave."

'Every person is greedy in this world.

Everyone wants more from their capacity.'

Laws

'Love is what?

When he created everything for you and you left everything for him that's love. God loves us. He created the heaven and the earth, the moon and the stars. Trees and mountains prostrate. And all other creatures on earth and the heaven. The angels, jinns, and the humans. The amphibians, Aerial, Aquatic, and terrestrial animals on this earth.

And these all are created just for you, this is Love.

Love that only God knows what he does to us. Some quality of God has been put into us humans. He shows great mercy to His servants and we show little. He loves his devotees immensely and we hate in the name of love. He knows how to give innumerable things and we cannot give anything to anyone. This is love in God's offering.

What kind of love are we seeing? Those who show favouritism from above and hate each other and abuse them. They are called hypocrites. And the whole world is full of hypocrites. Some true people know how to love truly. Know how to walk in the path of God. He who follows the path of God can never go astray in life.' I paused reading when she called me. I put her diary on the couch and walked out into the dining room. She decorated her dining table with a variety of foods. The smell of tastiness. I washed my hands and started eating.

I praised her food and said, "Your food is even tastier than others."

"Thank you so much." She grinned.

I noticed her, she was eating with her three fingers. She was chewing her food so much that there was not even the slightest sound of her chewing food. She was wearing a scarf while eating. All her habits were out of my senses. So I asked her, "Why you are eating with three fingers, chewing the food so late, and every other person removed their scarf and cap while eating because those headwear are disturbing while eating?"

"Oh my God Daksh, you noticed me so much than me." She chuckled.

I said, "Of course, These habits seem a little different. I mean strange."

She answered, "I eat food with three fingers because more food than required should not enter the stomach. If I eat too much with my fingers, I will appear greedy for food. I chew food many times so that my body gets proper vitamins and protein. Because by swallowing food quickly, the body does not get proper nutrition. And thirdly, I wear headwear while eating so that my hair does not fall into the food."

She was saying those all sound incredible. She was deliberate about living life properly and she esteemed all the things around her from the value of time to the value of food and many other things. Just because of this, she was happy in her life. But there is something that may change in human in their life and I wanted to know about her past.

I asked, "You are so philosophic that the person in front of you may bow down easily in your feet."

"Don't put me in sin by declaring this. We have to bow only before God."

"Indeed! But your words may easily melt anyone."

"These all are said by the prophet Muhammad the messenger of Allah. I only copied his words and followed him only in this world. And not only my religion but also the other 4,199 religions taught only good things to us."

I kept silent and continued my food. She completed her food and said, "All praise goes to Allah who grazed us with the varieties of food."

She thanked all of the little things in her life and enjoyed life. I finished my eating. "I enjoyed your dinner and I also got some rules about eating food." I giggled.

"It would be good if you apply these rules in your life." She grinned.

I asked, "Can I take this diary with me?."

She neglected, "No! I'm sorry you may read here or I will explain to you from this diary but I have nothing to lose except these words in the diary. I have written all my experience which my life taught me."

"I have a complaint against you."

She worried, "What?" Her furrowed forehead and pensive expression made me worried.

"Don't worry! I was trying to say that I have said my all past and you don't tell me anything about yourself."

"My past is like a puzzle. I will explain to you next time."

She said and she entered her bedroom. I understood what she said to me bye. So, I also went from there and closed the door.

Life is improper without any discipline in life. If you are living life then you have to live full of enjoyment and make sure there are some constraints and laws in living your life.

It was a bit late that night. Already, I'd been arrested a few days ago. My father warned me that if I was late then he wouldn't be allowed in his house. I didn't get a cab. So, I started walking. It is better to keep walking than standing still. So‹ I started walking and finding cabs simultaneously. My phone battery was 2%. My phone was going to die. I was running and walking on the street.

I got one beggar who was sleeping on the footpath. He stopped me from seeking food and money. I was not giving in the beginning. But, he was so stubborn that he didn't leave me without his money.

Anyhow, I reached home. I knocked on the door several times. I was ringing the bell frequently. They didn't open the door for half an hour. I thought they weren't at home. So I was going to ask for keys from our neighbour and then only they opened the door. My father tightly held my neck from the backside and took me inside his home. And he gave me a tight slap.

"I told you… I told you that you don't have to go anywhere. If you are going then you have to come back early to our home. This is not your club. We have some laws in our home. And you are continuously breaking it. Our building secretary called me and he informed me that this is not the hours to come in our society. If we continuously break these laws then we have to leave our own home." He scolded.

"Sorry papa!" I apologized with tears in my eyes.

"No dear don't sorry! Every time you apologized and did the same thing. You deceived us and made us settle in Delhi with one girl. And you were living in a live-in relationship. You asked sorry and I forgive you. Then, again you teased a girl on the way you apologized I forgive. How much time dear? How much time…?" He sighed.

"Not again papa!" I was going to hug but he pushed me away.

"Now, this time I won't forget. Get out of my home." He said calmly.

"Papa!" I sighed.

"I said get out…" He shouted.

He pushed me out of his door. My mom and my brother didn't say anything. I was standing out and he closed the door on my face. The voice of the closing door was so heavy that my heart jumped from its place. As soon as the door closed on me, tears started flowing, I was crying bitterly. I was walking gradually with the hope of my father call me from back. Gradually, I reached the main gate of the apartment. And finally, I came out of the society.

I was seeking an area for sleep. But the night was sleepless. My phone was dead so I called any of the fake friends. At least they would have helped me.

I got an old hotel, I had 1500 rupees in my pocket. And in my bank account, there were around 500.

Even the hotel was not getting me for a stay. I had enough money to stay in a third-class hotel.

It was raining and thundering, I saw a hotel. Which looked so creepy. The two-storey building was also covered with moss. I was completely drenched. When I entered the hotel, I saw the man sitting there as a recipient, asked, "Need a room? Will get."

"Yes, for one night!" I said, shivering from the cold.

"Are you feeling cold? You will get a good quilt!" He was talking very strangely. I paid for the key.

There was a tungsten bulb in the room. No good quilt, but I have to pass just a night.

I was feeling cold, so I removed my clothes and put them on the chair to dry. I was naked, so cold caught me. The blanket was also covered. Still feeling cold.

Three times I woke up in the middle of my sleep because of a cold. Every time I check whether my clothes have dried or not.

Finally, I got a sleep after dawn. I woke up late in the morning. It was 10:00 a.m. I borrowed a charger from the hotel and charged it. My clothes were dried so I put them on my body. And I saw Aisha's message she called me at the library. Rain was not occurring, so I stepped out with free-mindedness, forgiving last night's incidents, which was getting difficult for me.

There are some laws for living a love life. And those laws only make your person satisfied.

Mid-day

"Many angels and jinns were created by God. Before the world of humans, jinns were living on the earth. Then Jinns started spreading mischief in this world. They started disobeying and denying God. When evil had become widespread in the world, there was a fight between angels and Jinns. Everything was destroyed. And then God took pity on a very innocent little Jinn and took him with himself. And that jinn's name was Azazel. He was a very obedient servant of God and he was the best of all among the angels. He used to worship God a lot. God liked his prayer and prayer very much. God liked his prostrations. Azazel had worshipped the most to date. One day Azazil asked Allah about the book 'Luh e Mahfooz'. Everything about the world was written in this book. Everything from when the world began till the end of the world. Everything was written in this book. All fates were written. There was such a thing written in it that the Azazil started crying.

It was written In it that one of God's most beloved angels would disobey God and become God's biggest enemy. After some time, God created Adam and ordered all the angels to prostrate before Adam. This order was also given to Azazil but he refused saying that he would prostrate only in front of you and not in front of anyone else. "This is my order", God said.

"I prayed so much, I just worshipped you. And I, jinn made of fire, will prostrate before this clay effigy." Azazil growled.

God does not like arrogance at all. God rejected the worship of Azazil because of his arrogance. And he was expelled from Paradise. Azazel said, "I will provoke every servant of yours. I will try to make Adam's children stray from your path." God said, "He who will do whatever he wants, who will be my true servant, will never stray from my path. And I have made hell for him who asked for your word."

God who loves Azazil the most of all other angels now he is the enemy of God. Now, we the world call him The Satan.' Aisha narrated that outside the library there were only tables and chairs for students to complete books and other office work.

"Love is a trust, we can be ruined by betraying it." She said.

I asked, "What if Satan would have obeyed God's Command?"

"All this had to happen, the world had to be made. God wanted to make us understand that pride in love is a big sin." Aisha explained.

Suddenly the clouds started thundering. That disturbed our conversations.

When she opened the window to look out, we saw that it was raining heavily.

"Holy shit! I don't bring the umbrella." I chided.

"Even I don't have!" She mumbled.

We came out of the library.

Mid-day, at 2:30 pm clouds were darker than the grey color. Street lights were on. We both were waiting for the rain to stop.

Clouds were thundering and rain was endlessly occurring.

She prayed, "God I know you are showering mercy on us. But this time we want to reach our destination. Help us and show us the right path." She blew her prayers on her heart. And we paused for some time over there only.

"Why did we come outside?" I asked.

"Because I have to go for worship." She replied.

We were waiting for a ride. Suddenly, one car was running fast on the road, and there in the middle of the road, there was one kitten who was drenched and felt ill. She ran to save a little kitten. She took the kitten in her arms, car drove so fast that all the puddles came on Aisha and she was drenched.

She came with a kitten in her hand and there it's mom cat was stood at the roadside. Aisha dropped the kitten to its mom. That Cat held it in her mouth and ran away from there.

"You are completely drenched." I guffawed.

"So what?"

"I don't mean that! But you were waiting here for hours and you were drenched in seconds." I reassured.

"God wanted us to save that kitten. That's why we waited here for a long time. Now we have done with his command and I drenched too.

We are already drenched then we will get something more." She said.

Both of us were walking on the wet roads and in heavy rain. I shouted cab but the cab didn't reply to us and went from there. We walked some more ways and again we got a rickshaw but he also didn't take us with him.

When we were waiting for a cab, I saw my father staring at me from his car while passing in front of us. He was so aggressively staring at me.

"Why they are doing this?" I worried. She had to go home early. We were walking and walking till the bus stop which was 2km far from the library. It means we walked 2 kilometres. I was sneezing and coughing. I had a severe headache. I was worrying about last night. I didn't dare to go back home. It was because of my selfishness.

She worried, "Oh no, cold caught you."

"It's okay I'm fine," I reassured.

"No! you are not." She tensed.

"Okay, I will take medicines once I reach my home," I said, calming down her.

Then one cab came and we both sat in it. The cab was running fast on the road and the things were blurring around me. The same incident was revolving in front of my eyes. I got a call, "Now don't come back to my house. It's door shut for you forever. You always have to make your own decisions. Now I will never stop you. Do what you have to do But don't even try to come to the threshold of the house."

I put my phone on the seat.

"You are looking tense, everything alright?" She asked.

I nodded and gathered my courage to make my eyes open but it was not happening. I closed my eyes. I felt that I was in the cab but slowly felt myself in the air.

My hands and legs were tightly held by some people and my back was not at rest. Suddenly I opened my eyes and I saw that four doctors were standing around me and the four of them were tightly holding my both hands and legs respectively.

"Alright! Give him the injection and do one thing nurse, give him Citalopram." Doctor commanded.

"Yes!" She gave me and I ate.

"What happened to me, sister," I asked.

"You sleep now and don't worry." She ordered.

Doctors said to Aisha, "Does he have any kind of depression."

"No doctor. I don't know what's inside him. He was right some hours ago." She replied.

"Maybe he is hiding something. There are no foreign drugs in his body and no other substances which cause the conversions."

"Now what's further?" Aisha asked, worriedly.

"Because he has conversion features. This happened because of anxiety and depression. We gave him medicine to maintain his depression. But the thing is that he has to survive without any medicine. He was under observation for 24 hours. Now we examined that he had stretched in his brain due to depression." Doctor explained.

"What happened to him!" She lowered her voice and came towards my bed. Her voice was miserable and it was touching me.

"Aisha!" I called her. "It was my mistake that I don't have to hide it from you. I was being outed from my house. My father strictly prohibited me to come back to his house. Since last night, I was not at my home. When he outed me, I was roaming everywhere to find a roof to sleep. I got one hotel and I stayed last night there." I explained to her everything that had happened to me last night.

"What are you saying? So, you should apologize. "

"I seek forgiveness! But they remind me again to Forbidden to come home." I answered her.

"Daksh, if you don't mind can I say something?"

"Yes, sure."

"Your parents are your obstacles. Your own home is not good for you. Not because they hate you, but because they love you more than you think. That's your comfort zone.

You should live far from your house for some time. They're forbidding you to come home, but they will happily accept you when you go back to your house. They wanted you to see a successful person. If you are just sitting in a comfort zone you won't achieve anything in your life. I'm directly saying this because I do have some experiences."

Some words were getting me. They will be surely happy to see me as a successful person.

One hope raised in my mind was, "I will meet them when I will stand on my own feet."

Doctors came and said, "Here is your discharge paper. You got discharged. But ma'am you have to take care of him. Daily meditation as I directed on papers and most importantly don't let him alone at any cost. He may even commit suicide."

"Yes doctor, I will take care." She reassured to doctor.

"You are his wife?" He asked.

"No, no... He is my best friend." She chuckled.

And she looked at me and we both started laughing.

She took me with her home. She said while entering her home, "From now on you will live here only."

"But Aisha, won't be awkward for you?"

"That's the reason I said I beginning that you may live here till you get your own house and job." She frankly spoke. She put her bag on the table. She gave me another room. It was a fabulous room.

I rested on the bed for an hour. I fell asleep. I felt cold so I took a blanket and slept under it.

She knocked on the door and opened it, "Dinner is ready!"

I woke up and washed my face and hands.

We sat on the dining table. First, she was not eating for some seconds and then she chanted something and started eating. Her norms for everything in her life were different showing her in comparison to other people in the world. She cooked chicken tikka and dal fry. It was so tastiest.

We finished our food and she gave me mouth freshener. It was only 10:00 pm which was not late for me but for her it was late.

"Sleep peacefully here. If anything is required, make sure you will call me." She commanded.

"Sure!" I grinned.

"Good Night" She smiled sweetly.

"Good Night!!" I replied with a smile

She slept at 10:00 pm. She went to sleep. I also entered my bedroom and lay down on the bed. I didn't have my clothes and all. Still, I was managing.

Later I was feeling hot and irritable. I lowered the AC's temperature to 18°C. After some minutes still, I was facing the same problem. I put off my shirt. And I was trying my best to sleep. But I couldn't able to sleep.

Then, I slept on the floor. It was cooled. I got to sleep over there. After some hours, at midnight I opened my eyes again. I was feeling thirsty. I drank 1 litre of water from a jug. Still, my throat was parch. I went to the kitchen and was searching for water. Suddenly, one glass jug has fallen from my hand. Aisha came out to watch what happened. And she saw me and paused for some time. And then I apologized, "Sorry I broke it."

"It's okay! No problem."

She wore a long maxi dress and a short scarf on her head was tied. We both bent down together to pick up the pieces of glass. And we looked at each other. Our faces had just a 1cm gap. She neglected her evil whisper and began to collect the pieces of glass.

"What are you doing at this hour?" She asked.

"I was feeling thirsty so I came here to search a water."

She arched one eyebrow, "I have kept water in your room, Didn't you see in your room?"

She came along with me in my room. Pointed her hand towards the water in a jug kept on the corner of the table.

"My bad," I admitted with a lopsided smile, recognizing my silliness.

She chuckled, "Good Night!"

She went out by slowly closing the door and I went to bed.

Panic and suffering are more heavy on a person when the whole world leaves him.

Nightmare

The night was good until I woke up at 4:00 a.m. and I went out to look and saw Aisha on the prayer mat in the living room. She was in sujood (prostration). I smiled at her and thought how people are so religious even if they just wasted their time in spending these hours on God. After some time, I did not fall asleep so I got up for water, when I peeped outside, I saw her again in that same position still in the prostration. I went near to her and slowly I tapped on her hand to wake her. "Aisha! Aisha! Wake up, Aisha!"

She didn't even move.

Again, I tried to wake her up. She was in prostration but as soon as I touched her, she fell to the ground. I was scared, I took a glass of water and started sprinkling it on her, and she opened her eyes. Her scarf got drenched. She woke up, "Where Am I? What happened to me?" She was questioning herself.

I replied, "Don't worry, you are fine." I was calming down her.

"Oh, I got it! I was praying tahajjud (Night worship) and I got slept during prayer." She remembered.

"At this time of night, you were praying?" I asked shockingly.

"Yes! It's not obligatory but if someone worshipped at this hour then it would be more beneficial for him/her." She replied, with a calm voice.

"Ablution doesn't break if we sleep during prayer. So I have to continue." She talked to herself.

"You woke up properly or you will sleep more?" She asked while walking towards for ablution.

I hesitated, "No… I mean Yes."

She said, "It's okay, you may sleep now. Woke up before 8:00 a.m."

This time I got a sleep easily and it was the first time that I started dreaming.

I had a dream that:-

I was walking on the path which was going to the universe. Millions of stars and galaxies were around me. The path on which I was walking diverged in two ways. I was confused as to which should I choose. I saw Aisha coming towards me.

White color cloth on her body which only veiled her upper body and the lower body. Her waist was slightly visible.

She grabbed my hand and slowly she took me to the alley from where she'd come. When I saw myself I only wore one white colour cloth on my waist which was tied to my shoulder like a robe and one side of my chest and legs appeared from the knee. And we were walking and walking for a long time. Our lips were zipped and we could not able to talk. Finally, she entered one gate and I stopped outside. The gate was beautiful and the fairies around it were welcoming her. There was so much brightness on the gate and when she passed from that gate I saw her, her dress transformed into a long white colour gown and her open hair looked stunning. The silver corn crown and in the middle of it there was a sapphire.

But, I don't want to go inside it. My legs were stuck over there, I could not able to walk anymore. I was yelling, and shouting but nothing happened. I was stuck over there and the gate disappeared. I was weeping, crying, and started beating my hand on the floor. Suddenly, I woke up and saw Aisha standing in front of me. And she shouted, "You know why you couldn't able to enter inside?"

I was shocked, it was a dream or what?

How can she directly ask me?

"Because you don't believe in any God. I have explained to you many times still do the same thing. Why you don't believe it? I don't say, that you believe only Allah. But you can also believe in some other Gods. There are lots of names of that same God."

I was still surprised that she was in my dream.

She continued, "I know you are thinking how can I know all this? Because you were screaming and I know the interpretation of dream. You were screaming that you couldn't able to enter the gate of heaven. I understood what you were dreaming."

"Okay, I was screaming in sleep," I said releasing the breath I held.

"That's what I was thinking how could you know all this."

"I'm not any kind of magician that I know all the things." She chuckled. "Still, I am saying, believe! Believe in God." She always explained to me and I, the fool who never listened to her.

She asked, "What exactly happened in your dream?"

I explained all the things and she said by sitting next to me, "See, watching that you are walking in the universe it means you are feeling lost and lonely in this world.

And watching a fairy in your dream, means you are reaching your goal. Fairy dreams portend good fortune, just like angelic dreams do. Fairies rarely have negative connotations in dreams since they tend to be gentle. Fairies try to help and are a little timid. And fairies were not allowed you in the gate of heaven it means you are wrong. You are doing not well with your life and there's something still darkness in your mind and heart. Please erase those sins."

"What happens then if I don't?" I raised a question.

"There will be lots of punishments hereafter for the sins which commit in this world." She answered.

"How can I believe that there will be a life after this world?" I asked again.

"When we live in our mother's womb, we feel that this is our world. But an even more beautiful world waits for us outside. Similarly, whether we believe that there is a world ahead or not. But after this life, heaven is millions of times more beautiful than this. When we watch our palm through a microscope we get to see the big universe-type things in our palm. Don't you know about it?"

I was listening to her and getting understood by her beautiful words.

I grinned and let her words enter my mind and heart.

She asked, "So if you understood then let's have breakfast?"

"Sure!"

"What do you wanna eat?"

"What do you love to eat?"

"I love to eat everything."

"It's okay then, I'll cook pancake It will be a better option."

"Yes, please. It's been a long that I haven't eaten pancakes." I said, excitedly.

"So, it's done that today's menu is Pancake." She declared. "Do one thing, till then you take a shower." She continued,

"Aa... Daksh, I'm going to the general store, actually the batter got empty so I am going to buy it. Is it okay?"

"Yeah sure, you may go without any worries. I'm here!" I alliterated.

I entered the bathroom after 5 minutes she went.

After showering, I sat for breakfast. She readied a delicious breakfast for me. She baked a pancake with strawberries on it. Spreading sugar syrup and grapes decorated on pancake.

I ate and it was heaven. I never ate this level of delicious pancake.

"Mmmm! Heaven!" Eating pancake.

"Thank you so much." She grinned.

I again demanded one more pancake. I took a knife cut a piece and ate it with folk and it tasted delicious as I was eating.

When we do the same thing again and again it may be boring. But her pancake was so delicious that my appetite was tight and still my mind wasn't fulfilled.

"Daksh, I am going to school now. If you need anything everything is here only. And if you are going outside then keep the keys inside the boots which are kept outside."

I nodded.

"And, I will come soon because there's not many lectures of mine in today's schedule."

She completed.

"Aisha, I'm saying that I also wanted to join somewhere for a job. And today I have to search for my house." I announced.

"Do you have your master's degree?" She asked.

"No, I haven't completed yet! I said already that I am not going to college and from now I won't go." I cleared.

"Daksh, Don't do that! You have to go to college. Now you have moved on. So, go and complete your degree. It will matter more in the future." She explained.

I was thinking about this to continue my college But if I go there again, her memories will haunt me. Lest I get entangled in all this again.

"So, what should I do?" I asked.

"Wait for some days, decide what you want to do. Then we will book a flight and you back go to Delhi for your study. And do some job over there. Right now, rest at home and try to convince your parents and apologize to them." She grinned and went to her job.

I was walking here and there in her house. I lay down on the bed and started using my phone. I kept my phone aside and went to eat something from the kitchen. I opened the fridge and I saw one photo frame was thrown behind the fridge. I checked what is that?

And What do I see?

I saw the wedding photo frame of Aisha.

Aisha is a teenager with an elder guy. I was thinking about this!

Aisha is married. Where is his husband? Lots of things were roaming in my mind. I was waiting for her to come home so I asked. I wish it was a nightmare. But why am I feeling bad at all? Do I have feelings for her? No, she is my good friend and I felt bad that she hid such a big truth from me. I got my answer.

Love has an equal position for parents, friends, wives, brothers, sisters, etc.

_Hamza Khan

Osman (Aisha's past)

On August 12, 1994, I came into the world and lost my world.

My father was looking for the rickshaw in the heavy rainfall. My mother was suffering from pain. He got the rickshaw in a few minutes and he grabbed the Rickshaw. My Father's brother and his wife were helping her to lie in a rickshaw. She lay down and my father sat next to her.

They took her to the hospital but she fainted. The doctor took her to the ward and came back after 1 hour.

"Sorry! We could not able to save your wife.

Your wife has already died before you took her here."

My father deteriorated and he had a heart attack. The doctor treated him before he died.

He loved my mother so much. He loved her so much that they both died together.

My uncle his younger brother took care of me. He fostered me. And gave me love and care so much till his life.

When I was 10 years old. My uncle died in an accident.

I was sobbing next to his funeral calling him Dad and crying. My aunt saw me and took me into the bedroom and she beat me so much and said, "He was not your father! Your father already left you and also I'm not your mother. Cursed girl like you can't be my daughter." And she locked me inside the room.

The ground was pulled beneath my feet. I couldn't understand and I was locked for 2 days.

Am I a cursed girl?

I was cursing myself and I was locked for 1 whole day without food and water.

On the very next day, I was shouting and crying, "Mummy, open the door, please. I am hungry! Please feed me."

After 1 hour she entered the room and slapped me hard on my face "Don't call me mummy. I'm not your mother. Call me Aunty. I'm the mother of only my children."

And I said, "Aunty give me food. I'm too much hungry."

She gave me yesterday's leftover funeral food.

She used to give me household work and she removed my admission from the school.

It would have been better if I had known in my childhood that I was an orphan. Now suddenly both my foster parents and my parents were no more.

For 6 years, I tried my best to achieve my aunt's heart. But her heart was of rock for me.

Gradually, I understood the meaning of life in this age.

I started asking God for everything in life. My life was better after I understood that there's nobody for you only God.

I got a positive response from him every time.

Whenever I was in any kind of problem, I felt that he was testing my patience.

I used to go market for shopping. After coming home from the market, I cooked food for my aunt and both children.

One day, When I came back from the market an elder man followed me home. I turned back and saw that he stood and was staring at me. I was frightened and entered the apartment.

After some days, he came with his parents to our home.

They took a proposal for me. My aunt is immediately ready for marriage. I saw the man, he was 30 years old. He had a big moustache and beard. He was smart enough but I didn't like him.

My aunt sobbed in front of them that she didn't have anything and she was also an orphan talking about me.

So they were convinced and my Nikah (marriage) had done on dates and sweets.

I was only 16 years old. My aunt married me to that person without knowing anything. Except she knew his name, "Osman."

After some time, I learned that he had divorced 1 woman.

I didn't have my tongue to fight for myself.

No doubt, he kept me happy. He asked every day for one new thing.

He insisted on clearing the 10th board examination. And I cleared my 10th board with a higher percentage. He was so happy that he made me admitted to college. I took arts in college.

He used to live with me as a friend. He fulfils all my wishes.

At night, I used to teach him about the real meaning of religion.

He used to sleep on my lap at night. Our bonding was beautiful day by day.

We lived together for 5 years but he never forced me for anything.

We'd never had intercourse yet.

He loves me so much.

I was doing a BA in English. He supported me on every path of my life. His parents died between these years.

I emotionally supported him whenever he was in his problematic phase.

I have completed my BA and I got a degree. I was not feeling happy about winning, he was feeling equally happy.

He gave me a treat in a 5-star hotel. We came to our house. He settled down next to me. We worshipped together and thanks to God. I got up from prayer and sat on the bed. He settled down next to me and slowly kissed my forehead.

"I wish you good luck for a lifetime, dear."

"Amen!"

"Sorry Aisha, I was hiding the biggest truth from you."

"What?" I surprised.

"Will you forgive me?" He was stealing my eyes from me.

"Have you done anything wrong?" I asked.

"No, Aisha. I only did it for you." He said.

"What happened Osman?"

He woke up from bed opened the locker and removed one file from the cupboard.

He showed me his medical report.

He continued, "I have had a tumour in my brain for 5 years. The survival rate of tumour cancer is 5 years. Now, I have only days to live." He grinned with tears continuously flowing from his eyes.

I was surprised, feeling dizzy, and couldn't able to understand his single words after listening to his report.

"When we were marrying, at that time you knew this?" She rebuked.

"I was watching you for a long time (1 year). You had become my desire. Then my love. And when I saw my love in so much pain, I couldn't control myself and I got into a relationship. Already, my parents were finding a girl for me. I got a report and I was surprised. Firstly, I cried bitterly, not for this report. I cried for you. I wanted to marry you! Then, I thought at least for 5 years I would be with you. Not in this world, but we will live hereafter in this temporary world. That's why, I never touched you. If I had sex with you, then how would you manage all the things including the child alone? And I have done this flat to your name. This is your house now. I married you to take away from that house. The house of toxic people." He emphasized.

"Are you crazy, how I survive here alone for a lifetime?" I yelled.

"Don't cry or else God will not forgive me. If even a single tear is shed because of her husband, God never forgives that man." He placated.

I stopped crying. He slept on my lap. I was caressing his hair.

I also fell asleep while sitting. I opened my eyes, and I found myself on the bed. I woke up and he was not next to me.

I stood in fear and ran towards the hall, he was not there. I walked towards the kitchen, and he stood and made coffee for himself. It was a dawn, he asked, "Why do you wake up so early? Sleep now! It's 3:30 a.m."

"I woke up for tahajjud (night prayers)." I lied.

And I prostrated in front of God. I asked for the life of Osman and I cried the whole night for his life. And I was in prostration for 2 hours. I heard the voice of Adhan. I woke up and again went for ablution. I offered prayer to him.

He urged, "Today, I will make breakfast. A pancake."

"Oh, great!" I said, "Do you know how to make it?" I arched one eyebrow and asked.

He softly held my shoulder with his hard hands and replied, "Don't underestimate the power of Osman Khan."

"I'll also help!" I interfered.

"No, no, no, you may sit over there ma'am, order me what do you want to have now?"

"One cup of tea sir, and a good pancake."

I ordered teasingly.

"Sure ma'am, it will be good that you will never forget my taste of pancake." He hosted.

He pulled back the chair and said, "Sit ma'am!"

I sat and he started making pancakes. And he took it by putting honey on it with berries and tooty fruity on it.

I ate it and I felt bliss. "When you learn this?"

"I have been practising this recipe for 1 year just make you eat from my hand-made recipe."

"Thank you so much, Osman." I appreciated his work.

I wish you had eaten this to me for five years. We've never fought in these 5 years and our relationship was going smoothly.

After some days things were going to be good, it was above five years of tumour in his brain.

I thoughts my prayers are going to be accepted. But one day he got severe pain of a headache. And this headache he already faced before but he never told me about. He was used to hide these things from me.

But today he was shouting and crying not for the pain of his head, but for the pain of his love. He was leaving me and he knows me well. I drove the car to the hospital without any waiting for an ambulance.

He was not asking Jannah from God, he was seeking me with him in Jannah.

I saw love in his eyes that day. He was desperately loving me.

He was not saying that God eased his pain, instead he was saying God eased my(Aisha) pain after him.

He bewailed, "Thank God, I am dying before you. Or else I can't see you dying in front of me. Thanks to God that he provided me a wife like you who can hold my hand here and I know you only hold my hand in Jannah as well. Please, forgive me Aisha I don't know when you are upset because of me. But, God knows I always wanted you to be happy with me. Oh God,

Oh God, Oh God! I loved someone here in this world so much, I'm asking Aisha in Jannah too. Oh God, I want Aisha in Jannah too. I want Aisha in Jannah too." And he stopped uttering the words. I was crying listening to him as he stopped talking I stopped crying. I wiped my tears and wiped his tears. I took him to the hospital.

They sent back his body to our home. I didn't have the strength to talk with any one of the people who came for the funeral.

I didn't shed a drop of tears at his funeral. I was serving water to the guests who came for the funeral. They were talking behind me. Who is not crying for her husband?

I have broken from the inside and don't have the strength to talk. I have sent him the Qur'an 90 times in the period of waiting (iddat) of 130 days. In idea, we don't have to step out for 130 days after the husband dies.

I got a job as a teacher. Then, I understood why he hired me to get an education properly. So that I became independent after his death.

I did B.ed after 1 year of his death and started earning myself. I don't have his photos only this one I have! That's my story." She concluded.

I felt nothing in front of Osman's love. How he used to Love her?

"I am still angry with him! He used to hide everything from me. His aches, his problems, and even his love for me. I didn't mention him in front of anyone. You are asking so much that's why I narrated." She said.

Tears were shedding, I asked by wiping them, "Do you love him?"

"He loved me unconditionally but I did not. My heart melted to see his love for me." She snivelled as she looked out of the window, where it was raining too heavily.

I put my hand on her shoulder, "Don't cry! I never saw you crying before. If you cry who will console me on every phase of my problematic life." I consoled.

"Sorry!" she wiped her tears, "I was asking, so what do you think about your future."

"I'm going back to college, but not now," I admitted.

"Okay! Any reason?"

"Because I decided that I will go back to my college after tomorrow." I bantered.

She laughed too. "It's too late now! Go to sleep. " She commanded as she was moving towards her room.

She turned back and grinned, "Good Night!"

Her wish is a blessing for me. The therapy, her smile only heals me.

I lay down on the bed, window opened with the winds. Heavy rainfall at night sounds to me like the cradle songs, soothing vibes with the night. Thunder voices and the peaceful sleep that night.

"Love is not for exhibits, it has to be fulfilled wholeheartedly."

_Hamza Khan

Flashbacks

People were coming to their homes from the hostel and I was going back to my hostel. After three days, we finally got a ticket. Aisha came with me to drop me at the airport.

There was no luggage in my hand, only had the bag to carry on my back and shoulder.

She glanced at me, "I will miss you, Daksh. I attached so much in these days."

"You are the most important in my life, you saved me twice. First time from death and second time you gave me reason to live."

"We don't have any control of death and life, it's all in God's hands. We are the source of God to be around with people."

"Please, be in contact." I requested.

She nodded, "It's time to fly. Come on! Or else you will be late." I gave her one arm reach.

I boarded the flight and I reached Delhi around two hours. I didn't inform anyone of my arrival. There was no rain in Delhi. I found this city dry and hot. I ordered a cab and went to my room.

I opened it, there were things messed up in the room. The bed sheet had been thrown on the floor, and the glass and the bottle had been messed up on the dining table for one month. It was stinking inside the room.

I realized that I left my stuff at the door only, I took it inside and locked the door.

I started cleaning the room. Put the bedsheet inside the washing machine, wash all the utensils, and clean the floor which took my time more than one hour.

I rested on the bed. I saw a glimpse of her arriving in the bedroom. That was my delusion.

I started sobbing, I wanted to cry and shout but there were my neighbours would disturb me. I unbuttoned my shirt and removed my pants. I entered the bathroom, opened the shower and I was crying bitterly standing under the shower.

Every time, I supposedly her to mine. But she is not mine. She became of someone's other life. My tears were combined with water coming from the shower, I was shouting after opening all the taps in the bathroom. "I don't have anyone except you Krishna, why do you leave me? I always wanted you to be with me for a lifetime. Later, you were happy with me and suddenly you left me alone in this world. The times which we passed together, the love which we shared, the care we used to do for each other, I love you Krishna, still I love you. I love you from the corner of my heart, you deceived me my heart knows well, but still, he loves you. You have broken my heart Krishna, and I, with the broken heart loves you and will love you always.

Is there any wrong I did with you? Or I couldn't satisfy you to satisfy? Was I wrong somewhere? Question me, Krishna, why do you leave me alone in this world, in this house? We used to live with each other, right? I had left all my bad habits for you. I will forgive you if you will come back." I was talking to myself only standing in the shower. I moved out, finding a towel from my bag. The way from the bathroom to the bedroom was drenched because of me. I took the towel soaked myself and calmed down after showering.

I wrapped it around my waist and lay on the bed. After calmed down, I dialed Sanchit's number.

"Sanchit my friend, where are you?" I asked.

"Brother, first reply to me where are you? When you go from Delhi, you forget us."

"I came back, Sanchit," I replied.

"What? Where are you?" He surprised.

"I'm at my home only."

"Where is Krishna? Is she with you?"

I paused for seconds.

"Hello, hello" Sanchit reassured call.

"Yes, sorry, no... She is not with me right now."

"Okay, wait! I'm coming towards your home."

"Yes, please," I concluded the call.

He came in five minutes and hugged me,

"Bro, I was missing you so much." He said,

"You took a shower now, at this hour. Brother Cold will catch you because it is hot in the morning and cold in the evening in Delhi nowadays."

"Yes, I was going to wear clothes," I said.

And I sat on the chair. He got up and off the fan which was rotating so fast.

"I'm saying, that come to my house. After all, I will live alone here for 5 months till the end of the semester."

"Why? Where Krishna will live? Is there anything happened? Tell me, Daksh."

"Yes, the big problem fell on my head. Everything shattered. All the things got snatched from me. Even my father and mother left me alone on my consequences." I sighed.

"What are you saying? What exactly has happened?"

I narrated my story and explained everything from the start to the end. What I had faced. And from which phase I had passed through.

After he listened whole story, he was surprised. While narrating, my voice was going to be deep depressive in between. I had suppressed my sorrow in my heart. Not even in front of my best friend.

And we kept silent for some time. He hugged me and said, "My friend, you face lots of things these days. Why didn't you tell me about these all things? I can't do much more but at least I make you feel better in your difficult time. I will live with you. Whatever rent we will divide. Come on, let's forget all the things and wear your clothes. We will enjoy today's night in the nightclub with the ladies of Delhi. Come on!"

He was Insisting on me so much so that I readied for the club.

I joined him in the club. Lights were blinking as music was beating. Every were beautiful girls around us, and one of the girls was taken by Sanchit. I was also dancing with one girl over there. And I know that she intentionally put the glass of wine on my shirt. "Oh sorry! It's okay I will clean it." She apologized.

"It's okay, I will do it by myself."

But she was insisting. And she took me to the dressing room of the male. And said in a low voice "Remove your shirt please, I will clean it."

I unbuttoned my shirt. And slowly, unzipped her crop top from her back. I held tightly from her waist and started kissing ferociously. I kissed her neck and gradually moved towards her lips. Her hot and sexy lips attracted me. She was making herself more sexy and then I pushed her. I said, "Stop behaving like this in front of me." I yelled. I took out all my frustration on that girl.

She wiped her lips hard with her hand.

"Bitch!" I murmured.

She struggled to zip her back with her left hand. I moved out of the club called Sanchit and we went to our house.

The next day, I went to college. I was watching the ways where I and Krishna were having fun. I saw the Ice Gola shop where we used to eat. The trees were asking me about her and why you were traveling alone today. Where is she?

Suddenly, the rain started and I went under the roof. I saw her dancing in the rain. Playing with puddles and she was calling me to company her. I slowly step towards her and watch her from nearby. Suddenly, realized it was my dilemma.

I was drenched, Sanchit was calling me. I couldn't hear his words. I was finding her with everything over there in Delhi. The memories were so beautifully made between us in Delhi.

I can see her everywhere. I could only see her.

I returned from college and left behind Sanchit. And sat in the garden alone where I and Krishna also used to sit. The sky was clear, the sunset I was watching and I felt her beside me. I was thinking about her, 'You were not for me, yesterday and not for today too.'

I was watching the sunset till the sun set behind the buildings and I sat still over there. The weather was hit differently. Sometimes rains, sometimes sunny.

Life was being uprooted without her. Till I was with Aisha, my life wasn't reminded of her.

It was too late that I sat over there in the garden. I removed my phone from my bag and I on it. I saw, there were 10 to 13 missed calls from Sanchit. I call back him,

"Where are you Daksh?" Sanchit worried.

"Oh, sorry I am here in the garden next to our college," I replied.

"I don't have the keys!" He said.

"Fuck! I'm extremely sorry brother." I apologized.

"Okay, come fast. I'm waiting here for you."

I hurriedly moved to my house. It was 1 km far from our college. Where we used to on walking. But, I took a rickshaw and moved fast to my home. I reached my home. He was waiting outside and sat on the staircase.

"Bro, I am extremely sorry!" I apologized.

I gave him the keys, he opened the door. He entered the house without replying to me anything.

"Is everything alright?" I asked.

"That shit girl, Ankita is deceiving me."

"What are you saying? She is not like this. She won't!" I was confused.

He said, "I saw her with one boy. She was enjoying herself with her in the café. She does not even laugh with me. Whenever we went outside she kept silent. I was forcing her to live openly with me and not keep silent and I only warned him to not talk to others. But she doesn't talk to me and talk freely to others. And I saw her with a boy. I couldn't able to bear it. I hit him hard. We fight today. He slapped hard on my face. I beat him too. He forcefully pushed me and I fell on the ground. After that, I don't dare to fight back."

"Remove your t-shirt, let me see your wounds," I ordered him.

He removed his t-shirt. The shirt was stuck with glass fragments. Still, I removed some of them and the remaining were stacked on his back.

"What did you do brother, there were pieces of glasses stacked on your back," I said tensely.

"Remove it, bro!" He chided.

"Stop making this fucking faces in front of me and don't give me like this," I shouted. "Let's go to the hospital. Right now I'm removing it and putting some pieces of cotton on it."

I slowly removed all the glass pieces from his back by using forceps. And cleaned it with hydrogen peroxide. And took him to the clinic. The doctor warned me, "This is a police case. Still, I am moving for further treatment."

He had done with his treatment. He wore a sleeveless T-shirt. We back to our home.

I explained to him, "Brother, you may have some misunderstanding, or else Ankita is not like this."

"It means you do have to believe in her, not in me?"

"I don't mean that!" I explained.

"Let it be! I thought, at least you will support me."

"Don't worry, only I will stand with you if the whole world will leave you."

He hugged me, and I slowly patted him on his shoulder.

"Oh my God, I am not able to move properly." He said in a painful voice.

"Don't worry, I will let you eat. " I grinned.

He ate his dinner with my hand. I make him sleep.

'I am also in pain, but he could only watch his problem. I am missing you, Aisha. You supported me mentally. Every time you were there for me with every problem. Last month, I was facing so much pain and you were there for me to support me, to heal me. Here, some of your habits entered my soul, maybe! I am treating people like you do. Aisha, you are the best friend I ever have had. I don't want to leave you, never! I wish I could love you. But, I know you from a friend's point of view. When life was playing with me at that time you became my supporter.

How I repay the favours you did for me? Thank you, Aisha!' I thought lying on the bed.

Suddenly an idea clicked in my mind. 'Should I call her?... Of course, it's 4:30 a.m. she might wake up."

I called her, but she didn't receive the call. Again I tried, but this time she declined my call. Again, I tried. She picked up and said, "Hello, How do you do? Is everything alright Daksh you are calling me at this time?" She asked in a painful voice, which I did the mistake of recognizing.

"Yes, there is just clicked your thoughts in my mind so I dialled. And I know that you wake up at this time." I answered.

Then I heard a voice from behind, "Is it alright Aisha, you are talking on the phone at this time." A man's voice which seemed that he woke up freshly.

"Is there any other in your house?" I asked.

She didn't reply to anything and said, "I will call you later." She declined the call.

I had a doubt, who was he? Is there any family member of hers who is remaining and he rested at her house?' Breaking the chain of thoughts when he screamed in pain because he turned over on his back in his sleep.

I helped him to get back to his previous position of sleep.

"One of the biggest mistakes people make is to be suspicious of people. This drowns the human being."

Questions

Questions were arising in my mind. I assumed she was a bad character woman. Who lived alone. That she allowed me in her house without knowing me. I thought, she might let me enter some other man, but she also let me enter her house, even though she didn't even know me before. I was become so pure that I didn't even touch her. But, his intentions might be bad. If she is not a bad character girl, then that guy who was with her may manipulate her, touch her.' These thoughts were running in my mind.

Half of the night passed by treating another person and the remaining half went by treating my heartache. I felt so hard when I heard a guy's voice from her room.

I called her back, but this time she did not pick up the phone.

The alarm was ringing and I saw it was 5:00 a.m.

I slept at that time. I woke up at 11:00 a.m. My head and my heart both were aching the same. 'The girl to whom I trusted, to whom I shared everything of my personal life she couldn't able to share me just a small thing. When I asked, she denied it. It means she is wrong somewhere.' Breaking my thoughts of the train, Sanchit called me, "Brother, help me here in the kitchen."

I went to give my helping hands. I said, "Please, you sit on the dining table. I will serve you tea and bread. And tell me whatever you need."

"You were sleeping, so I didn't disturb you."

He said.

"It's okay bro…"

I served him breakfast. Then I went to brush my teeth and shower.

I took a bath and got ready for college. It was almost late, the college was at 10:00 a.m. and I was going at noon.

I did not have any idea, what had happened last night. 'This spiritual girl gave me a heartache. The girl who is showing herself so pure and spiritual is not like that she pretends. She is deceiving the whole world and me. The whole world doesn't know about her. They just leave thinking about her.

Not even one relative, one relative comes to her to ask about her. Maybe, they knew how is she?'

"Daksh, Daksh…! Where do you lose?" Professor yelled.

"Sorry sir, I was just…!"

"If you don't want to attend class then leave, don't sit here and don't disturb the class."

"Sorry sir!" I apologized.

The class was completed, I moved outside by hanging the bag on the shoulder and asked Ayaan, "What I was doing that Professor Vikas scolded me?"

"You were talking to yourself, even I didn't get your words."

"What the fuck you are saying?"

"About your fucking actions."

"I don't understand, whenever I was thinking about her. "

"Who? Krishna?"

"No, no, Aisha."

"Who is Aisha?"

"She is also a liar."

"Where does she live? Is she from Delhi?"

"No, she is from Mumbai!" I replied.

"She is your girlfriend?"

"Yeah! She is a girl and she is my friend. Sorry, she was!" I corrected.

"What had happened?"

"She became my friend in Mumbai. So we used to talk every day. One day, my father disowned me and let me out of his house. So, she supported me. And when I was ill she supported me at that time too. She was so religious when I saw her. She used to explain to me about love and spirituality. Today at 4 a.m. when I called her, the guy was next to her and she was hiding from me. I became always an open book in front of her and she hid everything from me. I felt bad, when she was with one guy, at night."

"Brother, Think a hundred times before accusing her. When a spiritual heartaches, that heart gives you the hundred curse.'

"Don't say, that you also believe in these stuffs. She was tired of being converted to her religion but she failed."

"Are you sure about your assumption? Because you don't even ask from her."

"It's okay, I will ask!" I said and took a phone and called her. She picked up the call and I started yelling, "Hello, Aisha, who was that guy next to you yesterday."

"He was not a man, he…" She was going to say something but before, I shouted, "Oh please Aisha, don't lie. I know you are not a bad character girl but intentions change with the person. Also, you are the girl who used to keep men in her houses. And pretending yourself as spiritual and religious. Krishna, Ankita, and you. Even all women are the same. All women wanted only men's fragrance."

"Shut up Daksh!" She shouted after collecting her whole strength. "Are you in senses?" Then her voice became rough because she shouted so loudly.

Ayan took the phone from me, "Assalam o alaikum ma'am, I'm extremely sorry. Yesterday, our friend got deceived by a girl. He has passed through the situations of deception from the girl. So his mind filled with hatred for women. Sorry on behalf of him." Ayan said, calmly.

"Oh shut up, I'm not sorry. What I did do wrong. I heard one man's voice. If she is not wrong then she should have cleared me last night only. But she didn't." And I took the phone from his hand and cut the call.

"What are you doing Daksh. Are you really out of your mind? You were not like this before we met."

"Circumstances changed the people. And I don't forgive who deceived me."

"She gave you all the things you need at that time. The time you were homeless, she gave you shelter for life. She sent you here because you should become a good personality man to have a degree and education power. And many things she provided to you. And you didn't even accept a single favour from her. You forgot the favour she did so quickly. At least you should respect her favours. What did you do? I won't forgive that person who deceives me. What you are doing?" Ayan explained.

I realized his words. But still, I had doubts.

"Do you love her?" Ayan asked suddenly.

"No…!"

"Then why are you jealous of her actions," Ayan asked.

"Please Ayan, leave me alone on myself."

"Okay Bro, do whatever you want to do!" He left.

I came back home, and Sanchit went back to his native place, Ramgadh. I was alone in my room. I roared. I was punching on the walls. My hand got injured. I was regretting or I was in anger I didn't understand.

After hitting the wall I sat down on the floor. I started crying and broke all the glass that was set on the dining table.

I had broken from the heart.

My wish was to kill her from my hand. My inner criminal was arising. The whole night, I was on the balcony of my house.

The cold breezes before rainfall and viral infection caught me.

My eyes opened in the morning when there was no sun but the cloudy weather. I hurriedly moved inside and again slept in the bedroom under the blanket. I off the fan and closed all the windows.

No one was there to care for me. And the one who got me, I lost her.

I slept for 9 hours a day. I woke up at 4'O clock in the afternoon.

My stomach was aching because I hadn't eaten anything since last night. I woke up with the other parts of my body aches. I felt as if a stone kept on my head. I was unable to wake but still I accumulated the courage to walk to the kitchen.

I opened the fridge and drank the milk which was kept in a tetra pack. I was finding other for eat. I got two eggs. I'd put it for boiling.

After eating, I went to the clinic. Took some medicines and came with other kinds of stuff of groceries. My expenses were going to an end. My mobile has been switched off since last night. Ayan came to my house.

"Are you fine?" Ayan asked worriedly.

Checking my temperature was high he was frightened.

"Bro, you have a high fever come on let's go to the hospital."

"I have been to the hospital and I bought medicines."

"Thank God, you did something good in your life for yourself."

"Ayan, I need help!"

"Yes, I'm always ready. Say what do you want?"

"I want a job in this city. Your dad is a business tycoon so tell him to appoint me as a worker in his company."

"Anything for you my friend. I will talk to him."

He dialled his father's number and called him.

"Assalam o alaikum Dad!....

....Dad, my friend needs an urgent place in your company. Please hire him.....

Ok, dad!.... Ok!.... Sure Dad!.. dad I'm giving this call to Daksh please talk to him...Here take it" I only heard his monologue.

"Hello, Uncle!" I greeted him.

"Tomorrow, go and meet our HR. Talk to them and make sure you will bring your BBA degree and other educational certificates. Also, prepare yourself. You are my son's friend it doesn't mean I will allow you in my company. You should have your skills." He said.

"Ok, uncle! Sure!" I replied.

"Best of Luck!" He said.

I didn't believe in luck so I just replied to him, "Hmm..." And he cut the call.

"Okay Boss, your problem gets also resolved." Ayan congratulated.

The next day, I went to the office. I showed all my documents. They verified the documents and took my interview.

It was fine and they selected me in the first attempt. They gave me a good package of 20,000 rupees for freshers only. I was so happy and I called Ayan's Dad and thanked him.

I was very happy. And I wanted to show this happiness to Aisha.

I realized this after getting my happiness back.

"Ayan, I wanted to talk to her!"

"Why you shouted on her last day."

"She should tell me all the things if he had any boyfriend behind me. If she had told me about him, I would not have said and shouted. But she was hiding from me that's why I got angry."

"Spit your anger now! And call her. Apologise!" Ayan said.

I nodded.

And dialled her number but she didn't receive it. I frequently call her.

"She is not receiving the call."

"It's obvious that you will insult such a pure girl she will offend."

"What are you talking? Do you know her?"

"Isn't it so weird? I don't know her still my inner mind supporting her. And you!"

"Sorry brother, can we change the topic?"

Ayan didn't reply.

"Live for today in my house." I continued.

"Let me talk to my mother."

"Okay!"

He called at his home to seek permission.

Still, I was considering her as a bitchy girl.

Perhaps a stone had fallen on my mind.

"I will be here for today." He replied after the call.

I grinned.

"Don't worry! She will call you back after some hours." He was making me understand.

'I don't want to!' I thought.

He patted his hand on my shoulder and said, "Come on! Let's go for a walk and enjoy some street food outside. You will feel freshness."

"I don't have a mood right now!" I said and sat on the sofa.

"Come on bro, come! Come…!" He insisted.

He was not tired of insisting on me continuously.

"Okay, I'm coming!" I said.

"Let me change my clothes. And you too, take these night outfits."

New Delhi looks more beautiful at night.

Walking on the Streets of Delhi was an adorable moment. I was reminded back my memories with Krishna. To whom I used to walk at night, eat street foods, and have other beautiful moments with her.

Memories were killing me at every step.

We ate street food. He showed me better options to eat in New Delhi, like general knowledge of street food in Delhi.

We had come back to our home.

I was still upset. The bed's mattress was cosy and soft but sleeping on it I felt that sleeping on rough land.

'Everything in the world is gorgeous but with lots of worries it feels like the world is a nightmare.'

Realisation

Received a message from Sanchit.

MESSAGES:-

SANCHIT:- I made the biggest mistake.

YOU:- What??

SANCHIT:- Ankita was not deceiving me. I was wrong. There is just a small misunderstanding created between us.

YOU:- So, what happened? She was kidding with you.

SANCHIT:- No!!! The one who was with her was his cousin's brother who came from the UK.

She was so enthusiastic after meeting him. And I thought differently.

I stopped texting him. There was a click in my mind. 'Am I wrong? She was not deceiving me. Maybe, I too have misunderstood. She was not lying.'

I was regretting it.

'What I did do? I don't have to do that. I don't have to allege her. How should I say sorry? What will be happened, if she is right? Women doesn't bear these allegations. And I told many wrong words to her.'

Then, again a message was received.

SANCHIT:- Now what will happen? I said yes to my house for that girl who they chose for my marriage.

YOU:- Deny back.

SANCHIT:- Not possible!

YOU:- We will do something!

Chats ended.

"What happened?" Ayan asked.

"Look once!" I showed our text message.

"Oh Fuck! Now, how he will manage?" Ayan gasped.

"Yes, how I will manage? Now, everything ended!" I said while thinking.

"What??" Ayan asked.

"I am saying, how He will manage?" I corrected.

"Yes, I know! Now, you are also regretting too. If your thoughts are right for her or not, aren't you?" He arched his one eyebrow and asked.

I nodded to reply 'Yes'

He didn't say anything for some time.

Then he looked at me and said, "Sleep now!"

The next day, Sanchit called me. I didn't receive his call.

I received his 10 missed calls. But, I wasn't have the mood to talk to him. Finally, I received his call.

"Why aren't you picking up my call?" Sanchit said in anger.

"Keep your ego with you brother!" I fumed.

"What the Fucking you are saying? I'm in trouble here and I am seeking help from you, and you!"

"Only you have problems? What about me? Every time you have the right to discuss your problems with me. Have you ever asked about my circumstances? From what I am passing through?"

"Your problems are with your two Fucking bitch! My problems are with the one loyal and trustworthy person. So, it's effective when we talk about a person like I have in my life. Not like yours, a bitchy girl."

"Shut up Sanchit!" I shouted. "Don't ever dare to talk on my girls from your abused tongue."

"If I don't talk about her then you have a problem. If I talks about her then you have problems. So, what should I do? You only said right now? You know, who was with Aisha that night? My brother lives in Mumbai. I said him to follow her and fuck her. And the day, you were talking from him that was my brother who manipulated her and done with it." He provoked.

"Sanchit, I will kill you! Note down my words, I will Kill You!"

I denied the call. I know he was provoking me.

Ayan came and asked, "What happened?"

I started crying. And hugged him. "My friend hit me from my back."

"Which friend?"

"Sanchit!"

"What are you talking? Again you are making a mistake."

"Listen to our call recording! In which manner he is talking related to Aisha? "

He heard and said, "He was in anger and you know him well. He said anything in anger. Ignore him!"

"I can't ignore him. His words hit me hard." Bewailed I.

"Do you ever think about your sudden blame on Aisha?" Ayan asked.

I kept silent. I didn't have the words to say.

Days passed, months passed with the same worries and problems.

I got a job, but still, I can't manage my problems. It means, money is not the only reason to be happy. Sanchit came to my room. He was silent. Fortunately, Ayan was with me on that day. Because we had a conflict.

I was silent too. We both just staring at each other. He came to me, "I am inviting you to my wedding. Please come!"

I didn't reply and stood quietly.

Ayan hugged him, "Congratulations Bro!"

He nodded and said, "I am leaving this room."

I was quite. He left the house. Ayan shouted, "Meet us in a college."

And he looked at me, "Are you crazy! He came with a good heart and wanted to invite you to his wedding. You not even replied to him."

"My heart was racing to talk to him but when I remembered his actions so I stepped back," I said.

Ayan took a deep breath and said, "Okay, let's go to college."

"I won't go today." I lay down on the bed.

"Today, there's our last day of college. And after 15 days there will be our exams." Ayan said.

"Fuck! I forgot in all these in a hurry." I regretted.

"Come on! Be ready fast!" He ordered.

We went to the college. On that day, most of the students were present.

The last lecture was good to attend.

Our class ended and all other friends were also gathered.

Sanchit's wedding was there after 2 months. I wanted to clear all my thoughts for him.

I didn't talk to him on that day.

My life was running too fast. In that speed of life, I, was managing my studies for exams, the internship and my part-time job.

Ayan was usually used to live with me.

He helped me with studying and other problems.

He was very nice and good to me.

Exams were going to be completed. I was prepared after the college. My parents were not calling me. At least for asking about my situation. But they did not care for me.

I packed my bags and went to Mumbai after college. I took holidays from office.

I planned to meet my family first and then to meet Aisha. I packed my bags and went to Mumbai. I reached after 30 hours.

I went to my house. There was no one at home. I knocked on the door for ten minutes. I saw lithe feet open and our neighbor's uncle came out and surprised to see, "Daksh, how do you do?"

"Fine uncle!"

"Dear, they are not at home. You don't know, they went to Bengaluru."

"Yes, I forgot!" I lied.

"Come and have some tea coffee."

"No uncle… Not now!"

"It's okay, dear! Come to our house."

And they insisted too much so I went with him.

Aunty brought coffee for me and my uncle.

Uncle asked, "How are your studies going on? Exams are over or not?"

"No, uncle. I have done with degree. Now, I am seeking a job."

"Where? In Mumbai?"

"No, now in New Delhi."

"Yes?"

"I got a job in New Delhi. So, I will shift there permanently."

"That's a great decision! But your parents?"

"Bhai is with them. He will handle it. I can't!" I said, drinking coffee and thinking that they still didn't forgive me.

I am done with coffee.

"Uncle thank you so much for a treat of coffee." I thanked them and went out of the society.

I saw my secretary, who was staring at me. He asked, "What are you doing here?"

I didn't reply to him and got out of society. I went to Aisha's house. She was not there. I called her frequently but she didn't pick up my call. I was tensed, I was a stranger in my town.

My old friends were also not available for me at that time.

I bought a room for a day and booked a return ticket for Delhi.

Till now, you might know me. I used to take showers whenever I was depressed. Because it's releases the dopamine. And this is the only way to make me happy.

The bathroom was beautifully designed. I can watch the whole of Mumbai from my bathroom. There were three walls of bricks and the fourth one was of glass. I took a shower first. Stood nude in bathroom

Watching Mumbai Lifeline. I was at the height of the 17th floor. The bathtub was overflowing with water. I closed the tap and added liquid soap to it. Slowly lay in the bathtub and I played a song. A smooth song was playing. I was thinking, 'Where she has gone and left me?

She is not even picking up my call. What happened to her? I already feel sorry for her. Why she is not getting this?'

I feel relaxed. Took a towel and I wrapped it around my waist. I dialled a hotel number and ordered a black coffee.

I had spent all my salary. I drank coffee and spent one night in Mumbai.

The next day, I had a train the next morning. I booked a Tatkal ticket. I woke up in the early morning and took a taxi to the CSMT. I got a seat on the train and I sat. I came with lots of hopes and was going with the thought of not coming here to Mumbai next time.

I was enjoying the view of the train. I loved to travel by train. There was beautiful scenery passing. I was enjoying that view. Night came, and I enjoyed the night's view too. The passing air was reminding me of my love for Krishna. I came while travelling thinking of her.

'Krishna deceived me. And what do I do? I alleged Aisha without thinking and hurt her. After knowing the pain of hurting.

Where she is now? She is not even at her house. Why did she shift from there? In just five months everything changed. From my personal life to my everything.

My wish was to meet her once in the life again. And wanted to clear her everything. I want to apologize. Why you are not coming in contact?' I was worried thinking of her.

I reached the next day to New Delhi. I took a rickshaw to my home. And called Ayan.

"My family were not in Mumbai and Aisha left her house. I don't know where is she now?"

"What are you saying? Where are you?"

"New Delhi!"

"What?"

"Yes, you heard it right!"

"Wait! I'm coming."

He drove rapidly to my house and knocked on the door. I opened it. He came and hugged me.

"Bro! Did you return? Why?"

I hugged him again and started crying.

"Everyone left me! My family is not there. They went to Bengaluru."

I left his hug and wiped my tears.

"But why bother? What I did do?" I asked.

"You did nothing. These are just bad times. It will be passed soon."

"Do one thing, come with us to Sanchit's wedding."

"No, I won't! I don't want to attend!"

"Come on Pal! Please, I'm requesting you."

He insisted on me and was trying to make me ready for his wedding.

He said, "I'm living here today at night."

"It's okay!"

"I'm not asking, I'm informing you." He chuckled.

I stared at him, said nothing and went to the Bedroom. He came following me.

"I lost my sleep," I said.

He said, "Sleep on my lap."

"What?"

"Nothing, just I'll give you the best therapy."

"Are you mad?"

He pulled me and made me comfortable on his lap. And he started massaging on my head. And said, "Sleep now!"

I feel sleepy. For some time I forgot all the things.

He was narrating the old story of his life. That was funny and beautiful.

And when did I sleep, I didn't have any idea.

The next morning, I woke up. Ayan was sleeping beside me. I made a tea. And started waking him up.

"Ayan! Ayan! Wake up, it's 11:00 a.m., brother."

"Hmm… I'm up. I woke up." He replied in a sleepy voice.

He woke up and I offered him a tea.

"What's your plan now? Will you come to Sanchit's wedding?"

"Again the same thing?"

"Come on! You are his friend. And we are planning for him to marry Ankita. In some days, he is going to marry. We have not much time to elope them."

And he explained me well.

"Okay! I'm ready!" I convinced.

"Pack your bags. We are going this Sunday." Ayan said. "And your ticket is confirmed. Which I have already done."

"What?" I surprised.

"Yes…!" He winked. And we drank tea together.

Whatever is destined to happen in our destiny, it happens. No one can stop it.

Truth?

Shiva, Manasi, Ananya, Vivek, Pranjal and I got ready for the trip.

"Where is Ankita?" I asked.

"She won't come with us?" Ayan replied.

"Then?" Manasi asked.

"She will come the day before the wedding," Ayan replied.

The announcement is done. We reached our platform. All were excited except me.

We arrived at Ramgadh, and Sanchit was shocked to see me. And my days of destruction began from here.

"Excuse me! It's time for your medicine." That old fat nurse woke me up.

I wiped my tears which were flowing from the side of my eyes.

They took me for the dressing for the last time and my discharge was done. The more miserable I felt for the first time after getting discharged. I didn't want those days back in my life.

More comfortable I was here in this hospital than in that prison. And obviously, every person felt the same.

My hand was not aching as much as before, but it was aching in my heart when I was sent back to the Prison.

I reached till the exit of the hospital and then the nurse, Aisha came in front of me. And she looked at me, in my eyes. I was staring at her and my curiosity to ask her about that day when she was hurt by my words. Ached after listening to the name of Aisha Osman.

Questions were running in my mind but the constables around me took me from there. They were taking me and my eyes were paused over there with the heaviness of curiosity.

I yelled, "Please clear me all the things! Whatever you know about Aisha. I want to meet her once and clear all the things."

And she remained looking at me. They pushed me in the jeep, as I was already fine.

The short route of around 2km seemed very long. I reached the Jail.

Vinay came to meet me.

"I missed you so much!" He hugged. "How are you now? How's your pain?"

"It's alright!" I confirmed.

"What's happening about your case? Has anyone come to you when you were in hospital?"

"Yes!" I said.

"Who came to you?"

"My memories!" I reassured.

He patted his hand on my shoulder and said, "You are not wrong. God is with you! He will make a path for you."

"You are also not wrong here, still facing this Dreadful Prison. How can I believe that He couldn't even help the one who is on his true alley." I stared at him, then continued, "There's no one except yourself. If I get a chance to release from here, I will take the path of loneliness this time. Even not the companion of money."

'Again the same thing, I was facing. The prison which I didn't want again, I got.

I prayed to God for the first time that they either be released or die. But, he....!'

"Daksh?" Someone shouted my name.

I slowly walked and went to that constable.

"You idiot! Come fast!" He shouted again.

"Yes Sir?" I asked.

"Someone came to meet you." My ears longed to hear this, finally, some had come.

My legs were trembling as I was walking to the meeting room.

And I stopped seeing her. Feet were going back, automatically. She shouted, "Wait! Daksh! I want to clear everything by today."

"I'm extremely Sorry Diya! I wanted to tell you everything, but you stuck me here!"

"I'm apologizing!" She down her gazed. And suddenly she asked, "What do you want to clear?"

I was surprised. "You don't know."

Constable shouted in between, "You only have 5 minutes to talk."

We ignored him.

"What else you are hiding from me?" She worried and asked.

"Sorry, Diya! But I wanted to know all the things about you. Still, you don't know! So, I don't want to say now."

"Daksh, tell me everything!"

I gazed down. And looked into her eyes, her eyes were curious to know the truth.

"We all friends decided to marry Sanchit to Ankita. He was getting mad at her. For some months, I was not talking with him. Still, I came to attend his wedding. And then I knew, that we were planning to elope them. Things were going as planned. Suddenly, he caught us doing that and he suicide in fear of defamation. I wanted to clear this thing at that time only, but you were not ready to listen. Even you did not come for a meeting once." I narrated.

"Daksh! Forgive me!"

"Why you are sorry for this?" I asked.

"The day before Sangeet, Ankita came for her love. She was begging for her love. Our father tightly slapped her. She said repeatedly, 'Call him once!'

But my father was not ready to at least listen to her words. She was crying. She falls on my father's feet. She loves him drastically. When I saw in her eyes, I saw the love for my brother." And she lowered her voice and continued, "My father went inside his room. And came back with a pump action shotgun. I came in between and said, 'Leave her dad. Please, don't do it!' And I make him understand. He put his gun down and said, 'Tell her to get out of this house.'

I said to her, 'Leave now Ankita! Or else, he will kill you and he will kill my brother too!' She slowly walked back to the exit door. And she promised me that she won't come back."

"What the hell are you saying? It means my prediction was right." I shocked.

"Which prediction you are telling of?" She asked.

"I saw her when she came to your house. But, I was not sure that she was Ankita only. Your other guests may also be coming." I said.

"Time is over now!" Constable shouted.

"Wait, sir! Our advocate is coming."

And the advocate came and released me. I got bail.

"Sign over here!" The police officer ordered.

And I cleared all the formalities. Finally, I got released. I said bye to my friend Vinay who supported me always.

I hugged Diya and said, "Thank you so much, Diya!"

There is no limit to my happiness. My jaw started painting when I was continuously smiling.

I asked, "Where are Ayan and the others!"

"They went back to their home." She answered.

"They don't care about me at all. They know that I am in jail and he neither came to free me nor came to meet me.

My punishment was bailable." I said surprised.

"That's why I was apologizing!" She said back.

"Why you are sorry?" I asked again.

"When I cleared my point of view that Sanchit suicide because of me. So that prediction was wrong. The main reason he suicide, was because of my father. He was not allowing him to marry Ankita. He ousted her from his house. So she does suicide. He got a call.

'Hello! I got this girl lying on the track. She died. Do you know her?'

'What the fuck are you talking? Give this phone to her!'

'Sir, is there any relation between this girl and you? I'm a forensic Officer the First first-responded officer at this crime scene. I got the phone so I found out that your number was dialled last time.' He said.

He wrote this all in his notebook and he kept it down on the window. But the book had fallen from the window and we couldn't find that day. When you were arrested, so we got his suicide note. There he mentioned all these in his note. He mentioned that he was dying because of his Father. My father had no option but to save his reputation and save from the stigma of his character. So he let you kept in jail. And Your friends don't know that you were in jail."

I had a big heart attack after hearing this, my heart paused listening to her story.

Again the heart ache by the woman. The woman who doesn't know the cruelty that passes from men's hearts. They never show, but they cry! They cry from his heart.

We were talking while walking. She said, "Now, I have to go now! And leave this city immediately! I felt bad when I found out that you were injured in the hospital. So, I finally decided not to give more pain to your heart. As I will be drowned in the sea of sins, and hell will be obligatory for me.

I realized yesterday, that I came to you to say Sorry! Please Daksh Forgive me!"

She was pleading guilty.

"No problem Diya! I will survive and anyhow I'll go back to my city."

Her eyes filled with tears and she hugged me tightly.

"My father should not know that I have got you released." She warned me.

She gave me one shawl. And offered me 10,000 rupees. I denied her money offer and accepted her shawl.

I asked, "Wasn't your love true for me?"

"Look, Daksh! We have faced many things because of you people. And I lose my brother. I released you because of my love. My heart didn't accept you as a prisoner. When I heard that you were injured, I was worried. I could not see you in this situation. Anyhow, I took the case return and did an advocate to release you.

If I take you into my life, then in the eyes of my family and the villagers, I will be disgraced. I have to take every step, so carefully. So, I am apologising. I'm sorry!

Happy Journey!"

She left me on the way. I chuckled a bit, "it's female's nature." And leave for my further journey.

I walked to the station of Ramgarh. My waiting was too long at that station. The night hours came and the people vanished from the station. I was hungry. I didn't have a single penny. There was one tea stall, I was staring at that stall. He looked at me and called me by waving his hand.

"Come! Come here!" He said.

I went near to him and asked, "What sir?"

"Do you want tea, here it is! Take it!" He offered me a cup of tea along with biscuits.

I took it from his hand and started eating as I had been hungry for months.

I was hurriedly eating. Meanwhile, he asked, "You look so decent and with a good background, why are you roaming here like a beggar."

"I, I am not a beggar!" I clarified.

"Then, will you give me the money for this tea and biscuits?"

"My condition will remain like this until I reach Delhi," I explained.

"Okay, you are from Delhi!"

"Yes sir!"

Then, I heard the voice of the coming train on the platform.

That's the train for Delhi. I rushed and boarded the train. I boarded on the GENERAL Section.

There was too much rush. I didn't get the seat to sit for a while.

I sat down on the train between the way to the washroom, in the passage. People were going there by hitting me on their feet.

It was night's hours and everybody was asleep. I woke up and watched people were sleeping peacefully.

Some of the passengers didn't get seats. So, one was sleeping in his bag, another one was sleeping inside the berth. I sat down at the gate of the train.

The train was running fast, I rested my head on the door of the train night passed and dawn arose. Suddenly, the train stopped. I opened my eyes, there was a beautiful lake in front of my eyes.

The dawn was beautiful, and gradually the sky coloured dark blue.

I descended from the train and I saw there were fishes in the lake that might ht be hungry. The movement of water increased as I came here, near the lake. I didn't have anything to eat them. I returned to the train. Where in the rush of passengers who were not able to sleep properly the whole night, I saw one man carrying bread with him. I asked him, "Can you give me this bread, in exchange for this shawl?" I offered my shawl to him. He said, "Don't worry! Keep the shawl with you." He gave me open-heartedly.

He got my point and gave me that packet of bread.

I opened the bread packet and tried to throw the bread from the train. But, bread was not reaching to the lake. So, I descended again and put all the loaves of bread in the lake.

And I saw there one thing which was shining. I went closer to it, and I saw one silver coin of the Mughal era. It was looking gorgeous, so I kept it in my pocket. And I saw the train was moving.

My running was slow when I was going to board the train. One stone stuck in my foot. So, I stopped and screamed. Even then I was running limping.

The train went far and I remained there.

'Love comes from admiration, not thought.'

_Hamza Khan

Peaceful Place

Time was spent gradually, the train was running in front of my eyes. I sat over there and waited for the next morning. It was cold out, so I wrapped my shawl over my shoulder. I lay down on the grass and watched the sky with three or four stars in the morning's dark blue sky.

The grasses were wet becausee of the frost. So, I woke up from there sat under the tree, and rested my back on the huge stone.

I fell asleep and suddenly woke up. What I was seeing, That there was a beautiful mountain after the railway track.

I slowly walked some more distance. I watched that I was at a high altitude. I followed the railway track and descended from the Mountain.

When I came down, there was one beautiful Dargah. I was hearing the voice of Qawwali songs and drums. That music attracted me and I entered that Dargah.

I was taking small steps to reach the Dargah. My leg was trembling, I fell and sat on the ground. The voice of the drums continued.

The tambourine waves were matching my heartbeat. One man ran and came to me, helped me to stand. Gave me a comfortable seat to sit. Then he offered me water to drink.

Music was going to continue. I sat on the corner of the dargah's wall and closed my eyes.

I had a dream,

I was walking on the path where I had already walked before with Aisha.

My mind was recapturing those way towards the gate of heaven.

I recognized the way to the gate of heaven. My body was covered with white clothes. And my eyes were finding Aisha over there. Suddenly, one gate came in front of my eyes. There were no fairies available instead there were some dangerous and terrifying men, those who were saying themselves as a bad angel who put the sinner in hell. And they took me with them, I was shouting. And when I turned back while entering, I saw Aisha standing with two good angels. She didn't help me. "Please, save me! Save me!" I was shouting. No one listened to me. And I opened my eyes.

It was the night. I was lying on the floor. I woke up suddenly and found the people around me. There was no one around.

I was roaming everywhere. My eyes fall on the gate of Dargah. It was closed with lots of threads and a lock.

Then I saw a woman, in the darkness everywhere. She had brightened the whole surrounding. I asked, "Where are everybody?"

She turned and answered, "You gave me the heartache, and you will know how it will be affected when a spiritual heart aches."

"Aisha! Sorry! I apologized."

She vanished from there and I woke up.

I found myself in the middle of the Dargah. It was not night. Everything was as usual when I slept.

Everyone was looking at me. To my actions. To what I was doing.

I did not have a place to stay. So, I stay on the street of the Dargah.

The visitors were fed the food to other visitors. The huge crowd was around them and they were sharing it with heartily.

I sat near the gate. I was hungry and I was not able to walk till there where they were sharing. However, I stood and went near to them. I extended my hand to ask for food. And the girl in a grey top and jeans. She veils her face from Dupatta. She gave me the plate and I thought that I knew these eyes.

And suddenly she contacted her eyes. She unveiled a dupatta from her face.

'Nurse Aisha!' I thought. My hands were trembling and the plate of food fell.

I was also going to fall, she came to me and made me stable by tightly holding my shoulders. And made me sit on the ground.

"Are you okay, Daksh?" She asked.

I nodded.

"You were imprisoned?" She shocked.

I replied to her with my full body's ability which was not because of not having food for two days, "Yes!"

"Thanks to God! Finally, my prayers have been accepted. Do one thing eat this!"

She prepared a morsel of food and fed it to me. And this is how she feeds me. I was feeling better after eating.

Then she asked, "How's this condition? How you are here? Explain me!"

"Diya who did the case on me took revert.

Not because she apologized to me. Because of the realization. The main person who is the reason for Sanchit's Suicide was not me, but his father. He let his girlfriend out of the house by insulting her so she suicide. He was in love with her and he also does the same, suicide." I narrated.

"Can I ask you something?"

"Yes!" She replied.

"Please tell me where is Aisha right now! How do you know her? "

"You had deteriorated her. You don't even know, because of you she suffered many problems in her life."

I realized my sins, "I don't know what happened to me that day. I was never concerned about anyone in my life. I did not know why I did that day. Maybe the satanic whispers through which I said to her. I realized my mistake after some days. But she is still disappointed with me." I cried.

"How she can't be disappointed? You made the mistake and made her disappointed." She said rudely.

"What exactly happened after I left Mumbai," I asked.

"Aisha came home after sending you. She was not feeling better. So she went to the hospital and on the way she fainted.

People surrounded her and took her to the nearest hospital. Doctors checked her and she is ill with cancer. The report showed that she was facing this thing for months. But she did not mention this to anyone." When she was narrating, tears were flowing.

The tambourine and drums were playing.

I got a mini attack on my heart after hearing that she was suffering from cancer.

She continued, "When you called her. First, she was not attending the calls. Already, doctors were asking her to call her family. But she doesn't have anyone. When you called her back so she picked up. In between doctor asked, "Who is there on the phone?" He asked intending to Inform. But you said to her something else that she had gone through rough trauma. She was traumatized for the next 10 days. She had never faced such an accusation. She is so pu"e girl. I don't understand why she took your words so deep. Because, when she came out of trauma, she only asked about you.

She forgot all the past things except you.

She was even denying me to accept me. The one who used to live with her after her marriage. I always supported her.

The reason is you. After some days, she recognized me. She told everything to me except her circumstances of heart."

"What else? Where is she now? You made me so tensed about her." I huffed.

"She is admitted to Mumbai's hospital. I went to her after leaving you in Ramgadh Hospital. I told her that you met me. And I found you in the hospital."

I interrupted, "So what she said?" and was curious to hear her answer.

"You don't know, how she would have reacted after listening to this. She was too worried. As usual, she was not leaving any prayer of the day. But she was only praying obligatory prayers. But listened to this, she was in prostration for the whole night. And the next day when I asked her, 'what you were doing?'

'Taking my curse back!' Aisha said worriedly.

'Which curse? What are you saying?'

'He gave me so much pain in my heart. I didn't say a single word. But my heart was not satisfied. He must have felt the curse of my heart.' And Tears wet her eyelids."

I had broken. My heart fragmented into pieces. And the realization was the hardest.

I started crying.

Aisha convinced me, "Seek Forgiveness to her. And first, seek forgiveness from God. Only God can heal you."

I was standing in front of God's home. But, I had never entered that house.

She went from Dargah and said, "I will be back tomorrow. Dargah don't sleep. It is the busiest place. Manage for today, I will come tomorrow. I'm sorry but my husband won't let you stay in our house."

"It is okay! I will manage here." I was going to ask can I meet her, but she went away from there. I laid the shawl on the ground. I lay down on it.

She was constant in my dreams.

Lying down I got up again. And seek forgiveness, 'Forgive me, Aisha. I have spent many days in misery. I want to meet you now.'

And I slept.

"Aisha" I was shocked.

She spread her hand on my head and I was going to hold her hand but she took back her hand.

She was in a red bridal suit. She said, "You can only touch me after Nikah."

"What Nikah?" I shocked.

"Yes! Nikah! But I won't be ready until you change yourself. Not for me! But for God."

"Aisha!" I shouted. She was going away from me and disappeared.

And I woke up.

I was thinking that she was talking about marriage in my dreams. I heard the voice of Adhan. Everyone was running to God.

'The whole world is praying to God, why I don't!'

"Because you are unaware of God's love. Once you get to know how much God loves you. You will win the sea with tears." Aisha Said stood in front of me.

I was going to approach her but she disappeared.

My love for her felt incompleteness without tears in my eyes.

Aisha, the nurse was entering inside the gate of Dargah. And she came to me with one bag. She offered me clothes to wear.

"Have you slept last night?" She politely asked.

"Your friend Aisha, did not let it," I answered slowly.

"Come on, take this! I have brought Kheer for you."

"Where is Aisha? Can we meet her?" I pleased. "Please, nurse! Let me meet her. How can I meet her? Tell me?" I hold my head with two hands to stabilize my headache. The severe ache was in my head.

"We will go to her. First, eat this! And I have booked the tickets for Mumbai. Today onwards we will go. Be ready, we are going through flite."

She provided clothes to wear.

With every step, I was walking out of Dargah, my heartbeat increased.

The trampoline and drums voices were beating my heart so steadily. People were entering the Dargah and I was moving out of it.

The rays of the sun were setting, and the new moon was rising. The first day of Muslim's month, according to the moon phases.

I was feeling peace inside because Aisha behaved well in my dream when I was in Dargah.

But the real peace was getting when I met her in my dreams.

Continuously, I saw her in my dreams, every time I slept.

We drove to the airport. I and I took our seats in the aeroplane. My heart was beating as I was reaching nearer to her.

The aeroplane landed in the lands of Mumbai. I was not in my subconscious mind.

We took a taxi to the hospital. And we reached the hospital. And I saw her from the glass window beside the gate of entrance in the ward. She was Sleeping on the bed. My eyes had frozen on the glass. My hands were put on the glass window, my forehead stuck to the window and my nose touched it.

Tears started flowing from my frozen eyes. She suffered because of me.

I could not bear to see her in this condition. "The sin I did and she is suffering." I started cursing myself.

"You also have suffered so much. Your life was not peaceful past 1 year. Every day you suffered like you hadn't suffered before. I saw you in the condition where you were not even in your senses. I saw you when you came to the hospital for your treatment. I know you are not happy. You haven't smiled after the day when you left Aisha Osman." Nurse Aisha said.

I was in the same position of watching her. Suddenly she started gasping and exhausted. I shouted, "Doctor! Doctor! Look at her." I was worried and the doctor entered inside for treatment.

Through the window I was watching her, they put curtains from inside. Now there was no possibility of even seeing her. After 2 hours, the doctor came out and said to Aisha, "Your friend will live only for one day. She is in the last stage of her life."

I started feeling as if the ground had slipped beneath my feet.

Don't know about death but if someone goes away without forgiving, then God does not forgive.

Spiritual Journey

"Universe is filled with seen and unseen things.

Everything seen and unseen is connected. Seen, which we are watching in our life. Which is happening in front of our eyes. But the thing which is happening in front of us but we couldn't able to see it.

On the other side, The universe is full of unseen things. Which has been happening to us for years but we could not realize it.

Love, until we don't see it, we don't believe in it. The power of love and the divine is unseen, the power of the Divine, the God, loves unconditionally but we are unable to realize it. Some people do believe in unseen things, believe in the power of God, they haven't seen entire in their life. But they died believing in it. The unseen things bless you and you can only see the beautiful moments in your life. Have you ever thought, about about where you are getting all these luxuries and peace in your life? Some people have immense wealth and fame. But they do not have peace and love. But you have peace in your life with limited wealth so it can fulfil your wishes and life.

This is the love of God. Which you cannot see!

God always says, 'Whatever help you need, ask me. I do not disappoint my servants. And whoever strays towards me, May I be pleased with this person and bless him with what he needs.'

Return to God. Indeed, He is the one who will give you peace." I opened my eyes, I was on the hospital chair and my head rested on my knee. I was feeling Aisha whispering in my ears.

I asked, "Nurse, where is Aisha?"

She didn't say a word so I got up to see her. She was praying with gestures.

"She won't leave any prayer in her life, now she is going to die, but still she is praying." Nurse Aisha said.

She had done with her prayers. Her eyes fell on me and she paused for seconds, she gazed down, and she started tapping tears. My heart stuck, I wanted to go inside the ward and wipe her tears. But, I was unable to.

I walked outside of the hospital. And there was one park, I went there and started weeping, crying for her.

Nurse Aisha came to me, And gasping, she said, "Aisha! Aisha!..."

"Yes, what happened to Aisha!" I worried.

"She is out of condition, Daksh! Doctors said, meet to her."

"I can't, I cannot able to see her dying, I will die with her. To whom I seek help! Who is here to help me to cure Aisha?

Is anyone there? Doctors raised their hands, There was nothing in their power now. Doctors are unable to do anything." I groaned, sat on the knee on the ground, and beat my hands on the ground. Nurse Aisha was stopping me from doing this nonsense.

'If no one is looking to help you. If there is no space, then there is God. He is always there to help. He never leaves His servant alone.' I remembered the words of Aisha.

I left Nurse Aisha in the hospital with Aisha, and I went out to seek help from God at his house. I started walking outside barefoot. Stones and thorns were not affecting my skin. I was finding God, everywhere. Someone said, "Your feet are bleeding." I ignored the wounds on my feet. I started running on the streets of Mumbai.

In the scorching heat, there was no effect on the bare injured feet. I had left my heart with Aisha. My tears were dried on my face, My red eyes were burning. There was a chain wrapped around my legs, which was not allowing me to go away from her.

In this big universe, where I find the true God. There are many Gods I was seeing.

I watched the group of Buddhist monks ascending on the bus. I was trying to call him, but he came from the front and asked, "What happened child? Is any problem troubling you?"

It was evening time when the sun set down.

"Aisha must have gone to God by now," I mumbled.

"What?" Monk asked pleasantly.

I started crying and they hugged me. And made me quiet and asked, "Would you like to come with us?"

I nodded. They took me with them and I sat on the seat of the bus.

"You know where are we going?" Monk asked.

I wiped my tears and looked towards him, asking, "Where?"

"Tawang, Arunachal Pradesh."

I was surprised and said, "Why?"

"You want to meet God, right?"

"But, By the time she will be died."

"If your intention is firm that after reaching Tawang you will become obedient to God, then she will be saved now. God will save her now. But your intention must be firm. Faith and prayer both are invisible, but they make impossible things possible."

"I had made up my mind. I got out and spread out. For God's sake. And to pray to save someone's life." I confirmed with a monk.

He smiled and said, "Sleep now! We have a long journey to Tawang." And they told them to start the bus.

They stopped the bus because of me. They proceeded only after my confirmation.

The bus was running, and I sat on the window seat and watched the night scenery. One child monk looked at me, I pretended that I was asleep.

"Bhikkhu!" That child monk said.

"Yes, Bhante!" that monk replied.

"But, you said we(Buddhism) focus more on teachings and practices rather than a belief in a single God." He expressed his doubts.

"Say silently, he is an atheist." Said Old Monk. "If we didn't bring him here he could do anything. He could have committed suicide, or taken some wrong step. If he stays here with us he will find peace. And Buddha will help him. Maybe the person for whom he came in this condition will also get well and this guy too."

"I will also become like you when I grow up. Like you, I will find out everything easily. How do you seem to know all these things?"

"Buddha's blessings are upon me. And he has given me a spiritual strength. That too after many years of penance. One has to work hard." He replied.

I also doubted, how he had overcome all the worries me even though I hadn't said any of them.

Listening to their talks, I hadn't changed my mind.

We had travelled 5 hours of way. The bus stopped and one young monk came, "Myself Chinshu! Come on, get fresh. The bus stopped for half an hour only."

I got off the bus and freshened up. He served tea to everyone, he offered me, "Have a tea!"

I held the cup from his hand and I started drinking tea. They gave me a cloth of saffron dye called a Kasaya robe.

I attired as they all were. They bought some other things to eat. We continued our journey. Chinshu came to me and asked, "Does bhikshu right?"

I nodded with the intention of Yes.

He asked again, "Are you in love."

I said, "I don't know whether it is Love or something else. Or I just cleared all her favours on me, or my heart became soft for people, or I became mad. I don't know."

"This is the symptoms of Love. You don't have any idea of what is happening to you. I too was stuck in this mud once. My life was deteriorated but God saved me and I am here."

I was curious to hear his story, so I asked, "What had happened?"

"That spiritual power I got after I lost my love. And I'm thankful that I don't get the love of creatures and get the love of the Creator. Years ago, when I was busy in the world prison and felt like the world was heaven. And in that fake heaven, I got a girl whom I considered the fairy of my world. In the beginning, my heart was attracted just for her beauty but as time passed, my heart attached to her heart. I was in love with her. I wanted her in every manner of life, on every value of life, I was helpless at that time. My parents were our enemies and my friends were not with me. Till then I wanted her when she said, "I'm engaged with another guy. You are not capable of achieving me. I'm sorry!" He threw her ring on my face and never came back. My love for her was like my love for God. My heart was of stone and became later of flower, for her. I realized then that the love was not for me.

I cried and was put in stressful situations. I had no option so I decided to accept my parent's decision. That was also like suicide. But the day before my marriage. I elope from my house. And I was running on the road, the bus was running behind me. They kept hitting the bus, but I was not going to listen. I stopped and let the bus hit me. But they took a brake. And the one guy came out, Bhikshu! He came as the angel came to help me. And he took me with him.

That God who snatched my love from me was going to give his love to me. And that is the surprise from God that he provided me. The Spiritual power of God. That spirituality through which I can travel over the world to spread Buddhism, to help people out of the stress.

And the spiritual power to connect my mind with God to talk and enhance my spiritual power. I am very glad that I am here with God, for God and for. God is the one who provided us the true friendship, true love, mercy, life, death and the greatest that he only loves us. In the love for us, he created the heaven and the world."

He narrated the story of his life and he talked like Aisha.

We reached our destination.

And it felt like a utopia. Bhikshu came and said, "Would you like to stay here forever or for a while."

I said to myself, "Forever." But stood silently.

"See, for this, you have to become a devotee of Buddha. If you will leave God in the path of your devotion to him, he will be angry with you. And we don't see God angry with their devotees." Bhikshu explained without listening to me. And that hits me hard, that he has the spiritual power of listening to one's heart talk.

I cried in front of him, "Forgive me! I will never leave God from now."

"Ask forgiveness to God!" He said.

They gave me a room to stay.

From the next day, He used to sit early in the morning meditation. And other religious practices, receiving a blessing, making merit, making a resolution, prostrating, making offerings, chanting, confession and repentance, and pilgrimage.

I had surrendered myself to God. I mostly do meditation. And after a long time, I got peace in my life. I was not talking to anyone except God.

This was my new life, I had forgotten all the worries and hard times that I had with me past days. I only knew how to connect with God.

Bhikshu came once, and politely said, "Dear, do some other things to make your God happy. We are in a world where we also have to do some occupation. Do one thing, colour the idol of Buddha or practice making the idols of Buddha. By doing this, your time will pass and God will also be happy with you."

And I started doing colour on Buddha's idols. Someone made the idols of Buddha and he used to give me to colour the Buddha Idol.

People used to be happy to see such beautiful colours on the effigy of Buddha. People were happy with my art. Bhikshu said, "You know why people are happy to see your art. Because you are doing this for your God. This is your power of spirituality."

Gradually, my idols became famous all over India. Every person was curious to know who was colouring the Buddha's idol. Because that was my spiritual work God was helping me on every path.

Someone leaked my video of colouring the Buddha's Idol.

We went to Sela Pass to travel from our monastery. The huge travelling distance I covered by walking.

We took a rest at our monastery in Sela Pass. The weather was cold there, and snowfall started. I peeped out from the window, remembering God in my mind and then I fell asleep and I had a dream.

When we are close to our God, God bless us with spiritual power.

Forgiveness

Violet sky and there was so cold that I was unable to move. Slowly the sky becomes an indigo colour, then it gradually increases the light in the sky. And it's a blue colour sky, I got up. I saw Aisha was sleeping on the bed which was situated in the sky. I saw her, and I was trying to get her up. "Aisha! Wake up, Aisha! See your Daksh, Daksh believes in God now. I believe in God, Aisha! I'm no longer an Atheist. Please, give me one opportunity! Wake up for me. Your spirituality took me here, at the corner of the earth. Not for you, but I'm living for God now. My aim for life is changed now."

She was not waking up. I was dying to see her awake. My tears were not in my control, waiting for her to get up. Then I got it that she died now.

My soul stopped, and my heart ached. The light blue sky turned into dark red. My tears stopped, my heartbeat stopped for a while, and the year drops were dried on my eyelashes. I was very vague that she died or not. But, I couldn't feel her beats and breathing.

I sat on my knees on the floor of cloud and hugged her, putting my head on her shoulder her hair was coming on my face by air.

When I woke up, I was lying down straight on the floor in a locked room. My body was aching so hard that I couldn't able to move. My head fell heavier, my eyes were blur I couldn't see properly. I was covered with a blanket and hardly I tried to wake up I got that I was sleeping nude. On it, someone put a blanket. I felt warmness before and gradually cold was catching me. However, I stood on my leg and the piece of cloth I tied it on my waist. But my leg was trembling and again I sat down on the floor.

What was happening last, when I did fall asleep? Then I got that I was dreaming, 'she was dead in my dream. Where could she be right now? But in my dream, I was confused that she was alive or not. My curiosity to meet her and to know at least she is alive or not. Even doctors were saying that she would die in hours, but how can we believe in them? The strength of taking spirit back is in only God's control. ' Suddenly, the door's lock opened and someone opened the door.

Chinshu entered my room, "Daksh, You got up." There was no limit to his happiness as he did not see me alive.

"What happened Chinshu!" I asked, confusedly.

He shouted and called everyone.

"One second, what has happened?"

"Finally You woke up!"

"I don't get it! Can you please clear me all the things!"

And he told me, "You were sleeping for 7 days."

"What?" I was shocked."

"Bhikshu of this monastery was treating you very well. You were freezing on the window, you were not opening the door. So we entered by breaking the lock. At first, we thought that you died, but your heart rate increased due to the cold. We removed your clothes and put fire near you. We were trying to wake you up for two days. Then the Bhikshu came and told us that our spirit had left the body. You are a good soul who can go to meet another beautiful spirit."

Bhikshu entered the room when he was narrating, and asked calmly, "How are you feeling now?"

I nodded with the reply of his question, "Yes! I'm good!"

He brought one glass of water and told me to drink a full glass.

"This was your journey. Now you have to get back into your routine."

"Bhikshu, what are you saying? I don't want to leave this peace."

"This world is not for peace. In this world, we have to face many difficulties in our life. Even the prophets did not live peacefully here in this world. You may have heard many stories of different prophets. They also have faced difficulties. This is a part of our lives. Go and join that part."

I cried a lot when I was leaving the monastery.

"Don't forget your spirituality. You have the strength to make idols of Buddha. Be continue with it and send us those idols." He grinned.

My ears were not ready to hear this. But, I should accept his every command. So, I maintained myself and tried to explain myself.

I leave for Mumbai. I left and turned back to my life, with the belief of God in my heart, with my love for God and with spiritual strength.

But the only regret, I wish I could meet Aisha.

I booked a train, I have a little money to reach Mumbai. I was in the monk's clothes. I didn't have my phone.

On my way, I got an old lady. She was staring at me for some minutes. And then she asked, "Are you that monk only who served idols and made beautiful idols of Lord Buddha."

"There are lots of Monks who do this. But, yes I'm also in one of them. I'm Daksh."

She was so enthusiastic after seeing me. "Where are you going?"

"I'm going back to rejoin my life. I had strayed from my path. I had forgotten that God is also in this beautiful world Then the world began to look beautiful. When I found out that the world is beautiful, then I went out to taste its pleasure."

"My eyes are filled with tears after hearing your words."

Her station came and she said, "I have bought your handmade Idols. Now you come back to this world, you will get how popular now in this world."

I couldn't understand her words. But, when I reached Mumbai. I got my handmade idols everywhere. I even got the one I coloured in first.

I reached Mumbai, now I wanted to first go to my house. There was one Rickshaw outside the station. He pleaded with me to sit in his rickshaw. I sat on that auto rickshaw. He asked, "Are you Daksh?"

"Yes! How do you know me?"

"See, your handmade idol is kept in my rickshaw."

I was shocked, that I was too popular in this life. I reached to my apartment. When I offered money to that auto-rickshaw driver, he denied it. My brother was outside the building talking to his friends. When I was talking to the rickshaw driver. He was surprised to see me, came running and hugged me.

"Daksh! Are you here!"

Their friends were greeting me. They never Respected me before. My brother took me to the house.

"Mom, Dad! Look who is here!" He said, excitedly.

Dad came out and was shocked. And hugged me tightly, and started crying.

"Forgive me, my child! I forgot you in front of my ego."

I lowered his humble hands and wept his tears with my palm. My mom hugged me, She was crying so much that she was not taking the name of stopping it.

"Don't cry dear, now he will be with us only." My father said encouragingly.

"Sorry, Papa! I won't! I am leaving this house. Whenever I want to come then I will come to you. But, I won't live with you all."

"Crazy man, don't be crazy. This is your home."

"Our home is not this world!" I replied to them and left them.

I wore a new Kasaya Robe and went to the Buddhist temple of Mumbai. Pagoda Temple in Borivali. It was beautifully designed and had good infrastructure.

I stopped there for one day. There was one Bhikshu I Got. He told me, "Bhante! Are you here?"

"Yes Bhikhshu, Bhikkhu sent me back to continue my life."

"You know Bhante! He never did like this, to send the worshippers back from the temple. But, there is something different in you. I couldn't see in your soul, but he did. Go and do that thing for which you were born in this life.

Come back to your own life. Wear like others, walk like others. God doesn't watch their servant's clothes. He watches our behaviour, heart, intentions and spirit."

"But, why you all are forcing me to come back to my life? I am happy like this!" I raised a question.

"It will be a benefit for you. I have talked to your Bhikkha! He told me to take care of you until she won't meet."

"Who is she?" I asked again.

"When she will meet, you will get it!"

I obeyed him, next day I went outside and sat at the beach. Where I and Aisha met first. The same day I was feeling. I was thinking of Aisha, our memorable moments and the beautiful times we spent together. How she used to teach me and I ignored her every word.

And I saw one girl riding a horse, too fast on the beach. I ran to the other side and stood in front of the horse. She stopped the horse by pulling the rein of the horse. She had a niqab on her face, I saw her eyes. I had drowned in it. I already recognized these eyes.

There was a strong gust of wind and her veil fell from her face I was going to faint with joy. My happiness had no abode. A ray of light suddenly came into my life. I did not expect that my worship would be so great. He brought Aisha Osman back in front of my eyes.

"Aisha! I'm shocked to see you! Am I dreaming again!"

"Am I dreaming Daksh! Are you really in front of my eyes?" She said, surprisingly.

"Yes, you are not dreaming!" We said together and we laughed together.

"Daksh! I have been waiting for you since that day when you left me for college."

She held my hand and said, "Now I can marry you!"

I was silent for some minutes. I couldn't understand her words. I looked at her, her eyes were shining with the moisture in her eyes. The shining evening became much more beautiful than the world.

My happiness had no abode. I was cheering like crazy from inside.

But I controlled my emotions and feelings, and said, "Aisha! You are saying this?"

"Yes! I was waiting for this day. When you met me the day after searching for me, since then I started loving you."

"What? Why didn't you tell me earlier?"

"Some things should say on it's right time."

"Aisha! Even when I started loving you, I couldn't able to tell you. Because, even I didn't understand what happened to me, why I'm thinking about you every time. The love that I knew, I could not able to define it. I could not able to understand myself, what I was thinking and what exactly I was doing. When the Bhikkhu sent me back I should have understood at that time only, why he was sending me back. He knew about all these things. He knew that my life would blossom."

"Your Teacher? Bhikkha?"

"Yes, Aisha! I learned many things from him after you. Like you, I also have the spiritual strength to pray to God and worship him with beautiful creativity to decorate him."

"That's beautiful Daksh! I was waiting for the day when you will also accept God.

I got you on social media where you were colouring and making the idols of Lord Buddha. My heart is full of love for you." She exclaimed.

"You are so sweet, Aisha! You have accepted me. I am apologizing to you! I thought of touching a pure girl like you. I was going to defame you. I apologize." I sobbed.

"I have forgiven you, Daksh. I never wished bad for you. Always praying for you.

Even Hakeem Luqman does not have the cure for doubt. You deliberately had a little doubt. I am the crazy one who was thinking about so many things.

Don't worry! I forgive you." She apologized to me.

I hugged her. She hugged me back.

Forgiveness is the beauty of human nature.

Ambiguous Wedding

Woefully, Nurse Aisha was not here with us. I wish she was with us right now. She has supported me every step of the way. She would be happy on our wedding day. The hours of marriage were near. She called me the next day at the masjid.

The clouds were beautiful outside, the sun was hiding behind the sky every few minutes.

The day was beautifully created for us.

I was already inside the mosque, she entered in a blue and golden colour suit. She was wearing the niqab, her eyes were shining. She came and sat next to me. Priest started the rituals of marriage.

We made this marriage with God as a witness. I Paid Meher (a bride wealth obligation) with a palm. The marriage was solemnized, and we signed the marriage papers.

And so the marriage was consummated. As if the incomplete dreams are fulfilled.

Angels were praying, God was showering His mercy. Love was connected. Love had begun. She did not express, she openly told the meaning of love. It was a relief to win love after losing so much, Had spent some time in persecution, now it seemed as if nothing had happened. All was forgotten.

God blessed me with a beautiful truth for the first time in my life.

The day of marriage was something different, where the richness I felt that day even without a single penny in my pocket.

We have come out of the mosque.

"Congratulations to you, Daksh!" She congratulated.

I congratulated her back.

She hugged me and I kissed her forehead.

"Now we are going to marry according to your religion." She said.

"No! It's okay! We have done with our marriage. I am so happy that you are in my Nikah now." I grinned holding both hands.

She insisted, "The hessian will be happened, go to the astrologer and talk about our marriage."

"No need! Come on! We will take the blessings of our Monk, Bhikkhu." I explained.

Then we went to Pagoda temple. Monk gave us the blessings and completed our wedding with a prayer and lama. Then he gave us a religious drink, madman.

We went out, and I asked, "Where we will live?"

"I bought one house and sold an old one. The house is in Kashmir. We will live alone there without anyone disturbance. We will do our work. You, keep doing your business of making idols. Don't lose it. This is your spirituality. I will do my work and will worship my God."

"Can I ask you something? What's your spiritual strength? You are so a spiritual girl who always worships and prays to God. God must have given you some spirituality for this worship. I have heard that God gives spiritual strength to his close servant."

"Daksh! I will tell you! But, I have already said, Some things will be known only in time."

I shook my head and said, "How we will go to Jammu."

"Flight is booked, we will reach out home tonight."

She gave me another surprise.

The plane landed in Kashmir after two and a half hours. We completed our checking and took our bags back.

She was so glad, I saw her. Her smile was constant since we took off from Mumbai to Jammu Airport.

We hired a cab outside the Jammu Airport to Pahalgam. It was not late night, still 7:00 p.m.

I asked from cab driver, "How much time will take us to reach Pahalgam?"

"More than 6 hours." He replied.

I was surprised, but we have started our journey for Pahalgam.

Aisha said, "Can we stop for our dinner?"

"Sure ma'am, in 10 minutes of way, there is one restaurant."

He drove to the restaurant and stopped the cab over there.

I got out of the car and opened the door on her side. I took her by the hand and let her down from the car.

She looked at me and grinned. We went inside the restaurant and ate dinner. Rested for half an hour and continued our journey.

We were not talking the whole way. I slowly put my head on her lap and slept.

The car was running from the darkness.

My eyes were closed, suddenly the car took a break and I got up.

"Yes Daksh! Everything is fine! You sleep!" She said soothingly.

"What exactly happened?" I asked to clear my doubts.

"The leopard was there, crossing the road." Driver said.

"That's cool!" I said.

"We will reach in some hours. The way is full of rocks, mountains and animals. But I will take care of you."

I shook my head and turned to Aisha, "Won't you sleep? Now, you take a nap."

"Daksh! I slept after you took a nap."

I grinned. She rested her head on my shoulder and hold my arms.

I feel heaven when she puts her head on my shoulder.

The car was running in the mountainous areas, and we could not able to see the view from outside, but it was visible that we were at a high altitude.

Temperature was decreasing as we were running further.

I removed my shawl from my right shoulder and put on her.

The car took a turn, she woke up.

I looked at her and hugged her. Then, she put her head on my lap.

I wish this time would pause. I loved the journey more than the destination. That journey was stunningly passed.

I rested my head on the seat and slept.

"Sir! We have reached the Pahalgam." Said Driver.

"On that valley, there is one house. Take the car over there." Aisha directed the way.

Finally, we reached our house. The house was made of wood. The lanterns were hung outside the house.

It was a floor house and a 10-meter yard in front of the house, was covered with wooden fences.

"The gorgeous wooden house, I loved it." I appreciated.

When we entered, there was one beautiful idol of Buddha.

The house was also gorgeous from the inside.

It is of 2BHK house. I kissed her forehead and appreciated her.

I held her shoulder by my right hand and entered our bedroom.

First, She did ablution and prayed to God.

On the third night, she worshipped God.

She spread the prayer mat on the floor and stood for the prayer.

She folded the prayer mat after being done with the prayer.

I sat beside her, we raised our hands to pray.

She removed her scarf and sat on the bed. Light the diya kept the right side of the bed on the table.

She silently sat on the bed. My heartbeat was going too fast.

She was sitting in front of me. I looked at her for the first time in so long. Even the dawn came while seeing her. She was so beautiful. She ate the whole world's beauty. I had already seen her, her beauty. But she was never the beauty she was looking on her wedding day, today.

My whole spirit was lost in her.

She was in a red and golden colour salwar kameez.

"You are so stunning, so gorgeous." I appreciated looking into her eyes.

"I have never let anyone see so far in my eyes. Not even Osman." She said.

"I have never seen this beauty in my whole life."

"After marriage, the beauty fulfils the bride and completes the faith of the Groom, bringing happiness. That's why the wedding is the beautiful ritual in every religion."

"But, you are so gorgeous. You shine so bright in my eyes. I couldn't able to see you as you are the sun in front of my eyes."

I was not tired of seeing her, watching her in front of my eyes.

When I saw her first, I couldn't recognize her beauty. But, now her beauty was making me faint.

I hold her hands, the bangles were lucky to have in her hands. The lipstick was the luckiest as it was on her lips.

And I was dreaming her lips on my lips. She came close to me. Gradually, decorated her lips on my lips.

I was feeling unconscious, even though I had already kissed many girls in my past.

But, today when she was kissing me, I felt warmness in the cold heaven. My feet were on the floor, I sat on the bed. Both legs were on the bed.

She moved back and raised her both hands to pray, she whispered the dua, "God! Bless us with happiness for a lifetime in this world and hereafter, Amen!"

She spread her dua's hands on her face.

And the voice of Azaan came to hear.

I rolled my eyes, and said, "Your Prayer's time is there you continue with it. I'm going for meditation."

"You should sleep today. Even, after Fajr prayer I will also go to sleep."

"No, sacrificing in the path of God is better. Worshipping is better than sleep."

She agreed with me, "Indeed!"

I changed my clothes and went to worshipping Lord Buddha.

I sat on the floor in front of Lord Buddha and meditated for hours. I felt sleepy. But I was controlling my sleep in between the meditation.

But, meditating with the focus on God was awakening me. After hours of meditation, I fall asleep.

I was in my Kasaya Robe, walking on the path that was going to the bliss.

My eyes went to the gate of eternity, where the Aisha stood in a white colour gown, waiting for me to enter with her.

Angels were welcoming us to enter it.

My steps were not fast for her. I was going to walk fast to reach early.

Her beauty was shining more than her beauty in the real world.

I don't know what happened, our souls started to fly in the universe. Started moving in a circular motion. Then our soul attached and I woke up.

I was confused, about what had happened in my dream today.

When I saw outside, it was night. I have been sleeping since the afternoon.

My stomach was aching from the hunger. Anyhow I stood on my legs, which were trembling.

With the support of my full body, I entered my bedroom.

I was surprised to see her sleep in the white colour gown. The same one she wears in my dream too.

She was sleeping, so I didn't disturb her. When I was going out, she called me from back, "Daksh! Where are you going?"

"I… I was going to eat something, I feel hungry."

"I'm extremely Sorry, I was also sleeping. So, I forgot to make any food."

"We will do our dinner outside today."

"Is there any shop open at this time?"

"What is the time?"

"It's 12:30 right now!"

"Oh My God, I was sleeping so long."

"Even, I too, was sleeping so long." Aisha regretted.

"It's okay! We will eat tomorrow."

"No! I will make some arrangements." She removed the tomatoes, carrots and cabbage. Make a salad, and sprinkle the salt on it. And we ate the salad.

"I forgot to fit the gas cylinder, I will call the serviceman of this village to do with all the pending work."

"It's okay! I will do all these things by tomorrow."

"Can I ask you one thing?" She asked.

"Yes!"

"Where is your friend, Ayan?"

"I don't know! Have you ever think where he is now?"

"Previously, I didn't care of him. Then I forgave him. And now I have forgotten him." I cleared.

"For which mistake, you forgave him."

"If there's one, so I talk. He made thousands of mistakes."

"You don't have to blame anyone without knowing. What exactly he had done with you?" She asked again.

"When I was in lock-up, he didn't come to meet me, to know my condition, circumstances. And he knew that I was not the reason for Sanchit's Suicide. But he never took my side of saving me. I don't know where he is now. I don't want to know?"

"It's okay! But remember one thing, he is not your sinner." She said calmly.

"You know where he is now?"

"Yes!"

"Where?" I asked.

And after listening to her, my world snatched beneath my feet.

'some sins were ours which we blame on others'

Idyllic Place

"Xenial behaviour and good-hearted person I never saw like him, like Ayan. When you were imprisoned there was no contact with anyone. So he contacted me at that time. He used to be worried for you. He was yearning to from where should you get in contact with him.

He called me once I don't know from where he got my contact number.

"Hello, Is there Aisha on the the phone?" He asked.

"Yes, Aisha here! Who is it?"

"Assalam o alaikum Aisha, Ayan here! Daksh's Friend." He introduced himself.

"Yeah!"

"Aisha, Daksh is with you?" He asked.

I was confused and asked, "What are you asking? We have not been in contact since around five to six months." I said in response.

"Aisha, I have been trying to contact him for one month. But I'm unable to get in contact with him. The last time Diya told me about him that he left her in the hospital because of defaming or raping her. I was seriously surprised by what she said. And I'm trying to get in contact with him. So I thought he might be with you."

I heard her talk.

"No, he isn't with me," I replied. I was being so normal that I was not at that moment.

"Ma'am, whenever you will get in contact with him please inform me first."

And after some time, I got to know about your condition. That you were in prison.

Nurse Aisha came to me. I hugged her, "Aisha! Thank God you came to me." I moisten my eyes after seeing her.

Nurse Aisha seemed disturbed. I asked, "What happened Aisha? Is everything okay? So you are joining back here in Mumbai."

And she told me about you that you are imprisoned.

When she left, first I contacted Ayan. And then I got the breaking news that he is no more."'

And she whispered in Arabic, "We belong to God and him we shall return."

I started shedding tears. "No, No, Don't Cry!" in a soft tone and wiped my tears. I lay down on her lap.

"This is the cycle of the world. One day I will also go to my God." She said.

"I only have you in this world. Please don't leave me. I won't bear the pain of losing you." Wailed I.

"I will never leave you, after all, you get me after my lots of prayer and worship." She blurted and paused.

"What? I wanted to know about you, why you suddenly offered me for marriage with you. I was a bit confused since yesterday." I questioned.

'"Daksh! Your curiosity to know about the love, your excitement to know about me, your grief to lose your first love, your heart for the family and your heart pure for me.

These all are the reasons which created affection in me for you. Before it, when you were close to me that night when you dropped the jug of water I was attracted towards you. When you went back to Delhi to study I started feeling emptiness without you, And lastly, when you accused me I was broken. The day when I started loving you. My love for you was intense.

Every day and every night, I wished you from God. And when he listened to me, at that time I was in not in condition. But I thought that I would not marry you until you started believing in God. And thanks to God, that you believe in him. When you went from the hospital, I had surgery on a tumour. And it was completed. Indeed God is with me, he plans better for us. He saved me even though doctors had raised hands. But there was a scope of saving me they got and they did the operation successfully with the blessing and mercy of God.

And you lost. Again, I waited for you for 1 year. Asking each day from my God to bless you wherever you are."'

"I can't believe that someone loves me so unconditionally, that she is back from his death to achieve me." I hugged her. There was a candle beside us, I off it with my thumb and a finger. Darkness spread in the bedroom, I could feel where was her shoulder and her waist. I kissed her forehead.

She put her head on my chest and my hands were on her back. I can't tell you how I felt so relaxed when she was resting on my chest, I was holding my breath to not let her sleep disturbed. When I caught my eye, I didn't even remember.

One man who wore a white coloured Jubbah (a long outer garment), tied a white turban on his head trying to wake up, and after some time, I realized that he was trying to wake up Aisha. When she up, he started calling with him.

I held Aisha's wrist, and said, "If you want to go then you can, but remember, your love snatched me towards you. I didn't come to you. Now, you awaken many emotions in me, so please if you're leaving me alone here be careful, I'll be destroyed in a second without you for a One moment."

"I am still loving you, but what about him, the one who loves me drastically." She answered.

"what about me, I too love Krishna, unconditionally. I thought I hated her, but, Daksh's inner spirit doesn't let her out of my heart. I still think about her." I answered.

"I know this very well, but Osman he wants to take with him. When you will return one's true love to him, you will get back your love too." Said, Aisha's spirit.

"So you don't love me?" I asked.

"I love you that's why I am letting you go to your true love. I know you love me, but more than me you love Krishna."

When I opened my eyes, Aisha woke up too.

"Is there everything fine?" She worried.

"Yes, Yes,! I'm okay!" I answered and pretended to sleep in front of her.

I was thinking, 'What was the dream about? Where I was listening to my inner soul's voice, Which I don't want to believe,

I am deliberately hiding the truth inside me, and I am accepting the situation.

What is this dream?

Those who meet me with my soul, meet the soul of Aisha. I should say this to Aisha, only she can solve this.'

"Daksh, you are still awake?" Aisha asked, in a slumberous voice.

"Yes, I was going to sleep and you called me." I lied.

I woke up early in the morning, she had already awakened before me and had done with her worship.

"Aisha! I have a question, Why have we come here so far? " I asked after adding lots of confusion in my mind.

"The reason, I came so far from your house, is because this is my dream life to live with my soul mate in the beautiful nature of Kashmir. I mean you!" She grinned and I chuckled.

"Aisha, every time I saw dreams, you were there in my dreams." I finally said.

"When was the last time you watched Dream related to me? " she asked.

"Last Night!" I answered.

"What?" she was shocked.

"What happened? Why you are so surprised, Aisha." I asked, worriedly.

"Daksh, you were asking me once about my spirituality, remember?" She gently asked.

I nodded.

"I was not aware of it, but you usually used to in my dream. First I dreamed of entering the Jannah where you could not able to enter in it."

"Similar to this dream I watched too." I interfered.

"And since that day, whenever I sleep, I got you. Hence, it was a lucid dream so it was in my control. That's why I was explaining everything because I was directing my dream. These dreams are not getting me, the dreams came to you, same I got it too." She explained.

"Okay, I'm going for a bath, can you please on the greaser?" removing my shirt and placed it on the washing machine.

"Sure, you are my husband. Your command over the head and eyes." She chuckled. I grinned.

She was in the Kitchen. Cooking breakfast for me, of course.

After a while, I went to the bathroom and called Aisha, "Aisha, haven't you on the greaser?"

"What? I have done with it immediately when you said." She said, confusedly.

"Check, the tap water," I commanded.

When she came inside the bathroom to check, I held her hand by my right hand and closed the door with my left hand.

"Water is warm, let me in the shower," I said going closely to her face. She cleared her throat, and said "I have taken a bath."

"It's okay!" I whispered in a low tone.

She hugged me while taking a bath. Her clothes were drenched, and I was in my undergarments. I offered her a towel, she dried herself. She flicked the towel and then tied it to my waist. My eyes were on her face and her pretty smile.

I kissed between her eyes. She moved out of the bathroom and offered me a white coloured shirt and blue jeans.

"Daksh, we will go out today. Dress well!"

"Sure, Ma'am!" I said jokingly.

"By the way, where we are going?"

"Xanadu!" she said in response.

"What's this?" I asked.

"The idyllic place, there were no beauties which left. Everything is there to grace the gorgeousness of the surroundings. The stunning reflection of the bliss you will get there. Everywhere you will find peace and happiness. The mind will detox, and the body will relax. The place is in Kashmir itself. Aru Valley."

It was not far from us. As we are "one with our breakfast. We sat on our horse. The brown-coloured horse, hairs on her head and ready to run smoothly and fast. I sat in front of Aisha, she pulled the rein of the horse. She said, "Hold the pommel tightly." She pulled the snaffle rein and the horse started running.

I was frightened, her hands were protecting me from both sides. She wore a hijab and still rode the horse well. Finally, after tearing the air, we reached our destination. And when I slowly lifted my gaze to see, it was a heaven I experienced. I have never experienced such a beautiful before.

It was the same as Aisha told me about this place. Xanadu is an idyllic and beautiful place. I kissed on her cheeks.

"I said, everything is beautiful here." She grinned.

"Yes, indeed. Including you."

The place was incredibly beautiful with lush green meadows, the snow-covered area and snow-covered hills in the background. The Himalaya Mountain was fully covered with snow. The pine trees were as attractive as Aisha's. I got the tranquillity that I had been seeking for a year. I hugged

Aisha, and confessed, "I am empty without you. The peace you have given me since these days is unexplainable."

"Are you happy?" Aisha asked.

"Of course! You are with me, How can I not be happy?!"

She held my both hands with her four fingers and tightly held them by her thumb, looking into my eyes, "All greatness to God and All thanks to God. God brought us together.

When I was counting my last breaths, when you took one step towards him, he made you come to me.

He has dragged me out of the mouth of death."

We took a rest under the pine tree.

"Aisha, I wanted to ask one thing, can I? " I questioned her.

"Yes Daksh!" She allowed me to continue.

"When I used to be your friend, I never got that you loved me. You kept a distance from me. Ever since you loved me at that time. Why?" I asked.

"Daksh, the love story is destined by God. If we interrupted his action he may be angry with us. Love like

Yaqub A.S, (peace be upon him) did. He worked with her father to achieve her for fourteen years. And the love story commences only after Marriage. Before it, there was only Satan who provoked us. There were a couple before the prophet's time. Who loved each other. When Muslims used to pilgrimage around the Ka'bah in Mecca they entered its, sanctuary. A named Asif committed adultery with a girl named Naila. God punished them by converting them into the stone.

When God said it's prohibited then you should not go near that. And there's a reason he forbade us to be in a relationship before marriage. Because we get fed up with each other even before marriage.

We live in relationships that have no foundation. If you get married it may create problems after marriage. But if you do not get it, then you cry for a few days and start life by the way. Like your life was when you were with Krishna. If you love her then go to their parents. If she will be in your fate then she will get you. But you have two options. Whether you achieve within a permissible way (halal) or in a forbidden way (Haram)." She explained stunningly.

"How to get in halal and Haram? I don't get this concept."

"Let me narrate you one story, A man was travelling with a camel. He saw that it was his worship time so he entered a masjid. He saw one man walking freely so he asked to take care of his camel. He agreed to do the camel's protection. That man came out after worship. He saw that the man was not near the camel. When he looked at his camel, there was something he felt emptiness. Then he noticed that the pad which placed between the camel's hump was not there. He went to the market and started seeking for a blanket to sit on the camel.

He saw that there was a shop, and "e asked the shopkeeper for the blanket to sit on the camel. He showed the camel's pad. He observed that this was the same pad he had on his camel. He asked the shopkeeper, 'Where did you get this?'

'before some moments, one sold me this in five dinars.' He chucked, and said, 'I was going to give him those five dinars for the protection of the camel. But he got in this way.' It means he had those five dinars in his fate. If he would wait for some more time by taking care of it he would get the money in a halal way. But he had chosen the Path of haram. He will be punished In this path." She narrated.

Her every story Is meaningful. The darkness was spreading and the temperature decreased. We bought a tent for the campaign. When we entered it, there was a warmness inside. I shut the lamp. I kissed her before sleep.

When God writes, destiny is bound to happen.

And only the prayers of a true heart can break.

Yearned

Yet, no dreams were disturbing my night. The hardship I went through the peace I was feeling.

Aisha told me once, 'God says in his Book Quran that, verily, with every hardship there is relief.'

Aisha was sleeping beside me, I couldn't take my eyes off her. Her beauty increased as the days passed after marriage.

I checked outside whether everything was okay or not. So, I moved out. I saw there was a snow Leopard. Roaming outside the tent. Everyone was camping, and one lady who sat outside in front of a bonfire screamed.

He was running towards our tent. I was like someone gave me anaesthesia, and forgot the surroundings. Then a wood that was on fire fell in front of the leopard.

He stepped back, and I saw back there was Aisha. I was yelling to not go in front of it. When she was nearer to it, I held her hand pulling her back.

She looked in his eye. Slowly, lift that wood with fire and throw it far from the leopard. That leopard ran away from there.

"What you were doing Aisha? That was an animal, a wild one. They have no idea." I yelled for the first time at her.

"He was scared. First I tried to threaten, and then I showed it that I was protecting. They understand sometimes." She explained well.

The next morning, I sat on the horse with her. She was riding it. We decided to go to the Buddhist temple. We started our journey.

I carried two Buddha's idols with me. While travelling, we came to a village where Aisha was giving sermons to the people of the village.

"When you truly believe in God, it doesn't matter what is currently going on in your life, you just leave all your worries on God. Only he can fix everything. But you only have to believe in him. He loves you immensely. I told this many times to many people. We're not aware of it, how much he loves us. When we rely on God then he is happy for us. He is glad that their servants who don't even see him still believe from the core of their hearts. He showed the other creature, the angels, see my servant who never saw me still have faith in me, on prophets, on angels, on the day of resurrection, on life and death. Only the good deeds will be seen on the day of resurrection. No people who used to backbiting about us will judge our character. Only the God who knows all the things, the almighty who knows what's in our hearts. Don't think about others what say, instead think about how we will face God hereafter." And she was delivering her beautiful sermon to the people of the village. I was recording her from my phone.

She saw me when I was recording, she looked at me from the corner of her eyes. As she wore a niqab I couldn't see her chuckle. But her eyes smiled so beautifully that I noticed so well.

She had done with her speech.

"Why do they call you for speech?"

"I came before for the first time with Osman. The youth here did not indulge in any of the activities of God's worship, their parents were worried because of them. I explained to them to start their worship of God. So, many people back to their religion."

One teenage boy, who was around 18 years said, "Sister, here take this woollen shawl. My mom stitched this. She is no more in this world. She kept this for you. She knew that you would come back here for sure." He talked while holding the flood of tears in his eyes.

"Daksh he is Siddharth Pandita. The most naughty boy of the village." Aisha was trying to distract him. But she couldn't control and hugged him. He started crying.

She consoled him and accepted the shawl. "I'm here only Siddharth. Don't be disappointed. Your sister is always here." He wiped his tears.

We left the horse in the village and ordered a cab.

In some hours, we reached our destination. Shey Monastery. Where my Bhikshu came there. I entered the temple and wore my robe. And I met Bhikshu.

I told him, "My wife, Aisha Daksh."

"This soul attracted you when you were in a monastery. The beautiful soul where your spirituality doesn't even work. Even God wanted both of you to be married. The love for each other only in their heart, in their spirits is impossible in this era. The love of lord Siddhartha and Yashoda,

Prophet Muhammad and his wife Aisha. Love like them is never seen in this generation.

Where the love is stuck in the false promises and oaths. The love relies on sexual intercourse. The love which only waits without each other not more than forty days. In this time of false love, this girl accepted you spiritually.

God blessed her with life because of the one step of love you took for her when you came with us to the monastery. He never saw religion. God is in everyone's heart but they never know. And those who know they never forget God.

Your souls used to meet each other in dreams. Your lucid dreams technique never worked. It happened by the permission of God." He talked with us.

My doubts were clear as crystal.

"Child, the best decision is to live far from society. They never let you live peacefully. Everyone would raise their voice where the Buddhist Monk lives with Aalima (Female cleric)." Said Bhikshu.

She grinned, "Thank you Bhikshu." And we talked with them for hours.

We waited there till night at the monastery. I and Aisha came outside for dinner and we booked a room for our stay.

I was not blinking while seeing Aisha, I off the lights. I kissed her gently on her lips. And I took the blanket on us, higher the temperature of the heater. One candle was placed on the table, and I off it from my hand.

The next day, we went back to our home. I and Aisha started teaching in school. I was used to teaching higher secondary school. She taught primary and secondary students.

God was showering blessings on us and the day with full of blessings. Aisha was teaching in her class and she fell unconscious. I ran to her lifted her in my arms ran to the hospital. I got the news there, that she was going to be a mother and I was going to be a father. There was so much joy in life together.

I cooked the food for her and fed her. I appointed the maid in our house. For the food, I used to make everything for her.

But her health was deteriorating day by day. As months passed, she was not feeling well.

Seeing her sitting on a bed crying for health I used to worried every time.

She used to pray by sitting. Like old lady worships.

Still, I left no stone unturned to take care of her. The whole village was worried for her.

We went to Srinagar for the treatment and called Nurse Aisha. When Aisha saw Nurse Aisha she became so elated.

But her inner pain was not showing her upper overjoyed. Her eyes went inside. The dark circles were appearing on her face.

The people of the village used to love her a lot. Siddharth was crying outside of the hospital. As he has no one except Aisha.

Nurse Aisha came, and I started sobbing.

"What happened to Aisha? Will she be fine soon?"

"Don't worry. In her more than thirty years she never faced this situation. She never had intercourse with any another. She will be fine after baby." Nurse Aisha consoled.

She makes me sit on the chair. Months passed, and she was yearning as the days were passing. Finally, the day came. The snowfall was occurring. She was screaming because of pain. We called the doctor immediately. The whole village was waiting outside our house.

I was impatience, but finally, she stopped screaming and we heard the scream of the baby. I entered inside, "Aisha! Are you fine?"

"Here your baby, she is a Girl." I grinned and took her in my arms. I started crying seeing her. The same beauty was shining like Aisha.

"Aadab, her name." I grinned and looked at Aisha.

Her eyes were on us and she grinned.

"Aikya, her name." she insisted.

I smiled while shedding tears, "OK! I will call her Aadab, you call her Aikya."

"Give it to me?!" she insisted.

I gave it to her and sat on the floor resting my head and hands on the bed looking at my daughter and wife. I stood and went out to announce, "The villagers, from the beautiful soul like Aisha, my daughter Aadab came into this world." The people of the village were overjoyed after listening to the news.

Nurse Aisha came and said, “Thanks to God, baby is fine. Or else pregnancy after 30, the children may take birth with Down syndrome. And mostly miscarriage may also done. It was so risky. But it’s all fine.,”

When I entered the bedroom, I saw Aisha was sleeping. Aadab was sleeping peacefully with her. I came back without disturbing anyone.

I sat down put my hands on the bed and rested my head on it beside her. I got a call on my phone.

‘It’s unknown! Who can be calling at this hour?’

It was ringing so I silent it by pressing the volume key and moving outside the room to not disturb Aisha, and receive the call.

“Hello!” She greeted.

“Who is it?” I asked.

She started sobbing, “Daksh! It is me, Krishna.”

“What!! Krishna!” I was surprised.

“Daksh, save me! I want to back my country India.”

“What happened to you Krishna.” I forgot all the sins that she committed against me and asked about her circumstances.

“Daksh! He wanted to kill me now.” She sobbed.

“Krishna, tell me clearly what happened?”

“Kabir, to whom I eloped. He wanted to kill me. I had your mobile number when I called you. Now, saved me, Daksh! He took my passport.”

“But why he wants to kill you?” I asked.

“Because he got to know that his child Siddharth is not his child. His father is you. He is 2 years old.”

My head was spinning all the way.

“What I can do? I can’t leave my wife here alone.”

“He is your baby Daksh! Do something!”

“your demand is out of range. Sorry, I can’t help!” and I denied her call. I went back to my bedroom and slept beside Aisha.

I woke up with the cry of Aadab and I saw that Aisha was not getting disturbed by her cry. I called Aisha, "Aisha! Aisha! Why are you not waking up? Feed her, she's hungry be." But she has not opened her eyes.

I called nurse Aisha, I took Aadab in my arms trying to keep her quiet. But she was crying loudly. When I saw the door, I saw Aisha was going out of the door. That was her spirit. She was smiling and crying at the same time. Nurse Aisha came and started waking her up. But she has not opened her eyes.

I lay down Aadab on the bed. I sat down on the floor, with the silence of my heartbeat with the ache in my heart, my heart was beating so fast and my eyes were drenched with tears.

God puts love on our hearts, and God tests us by snatching our loved ones.

God and Spiritual heart

Zestless I became, I had no strength to stand on my legs. Nurse Aisha called a cab and took her to the hospital. We reached soon the hospital. Her heartbeats were not running, my heartbeats were going to stop. I had Aadab in my hand. Glimpse I could see in Aadab.

They stopped me out of the ward and they took her to the casualty ward. After, an hour they took her to the MRI room.

I got the news that she was alive and my soul returned to my body. But her condition was not good. They put her in the ward and again doctors took her to the ICU room.

There was a silence on my face. Nurse Aisha came to me and said, "Pray for her. Only God can heal her."

She took Aadab from my hand and was trying to keep her quiet. She bought milk for her and fed her.

My phone rang again, it was Krishna's phone, I had not received her first five to six calls. But finally, I received it it.

"Daksh, do you want your child to be killed? Don't care for me. But at least care for your son."

I was silently listening to her call.., "Look Daksh, if my child dies because of you the curse of my heartache will affect your life so hard."

"Please Krishna, forgive me. Why are you pressurizing me so much? I am already in a big pain of my life. The one who loved me so much in my whole life. Not even my parents cared and loved me, she did. Her love for me is so unconditional that my spirit is attracted towards her spirit. I already cleared the debt of someone's curse. But not now, I don't have that many guts to again face it." I requested with the core of my heart.

She denied the call. But, I also thought of her. She is my first love. I should helped her. And that's my child too. I was waiting for Aisha to wake up so that I could share this problem with her.

I sat in front of God, seeking help in this hard time.

My eyes were dried.

"God for me, for my love, for this blessing which you sent to us in our home in the form of a daughter. She will be alone, God! I'm asking Aisha back to me. We recently have a family. Oh God, I want my Aisha back. I know she's yours. But her life just had started. She faced a lot of difficulties in her life. Now it's her time to enjoy her life with her daughter, with her husband (I), and provide her more time to worship you, God. Her belief In you is deeper than the heart, deeper than her eyes. Oh God, you live in her heart. Cure her. Oh god, listen to my prayer and accept my prayers."

I got a call from Krishna again, "Hello!" I greeted.

"I got my passport and Siddharth's passport. Now, I am taking him to you.

I understood her pain and circumstances, said "Okay! You can come to me. But you cannot come back to my heart. Not even my life. Whatever money you need tell me I will transfer it to you." I said.

"I am extremely sorry Daksh. You are the best May all your wishes be fulfilled."

"Once you reach the airport, inform me," I said.

I heard that someone rang the bell at her house. She put on her phone without cutting it. I heard her husband beating. Krishna was screaming so loudly. One person pushed another person so hard that I could hear the sound of him falling on the wall. I was shouting from here while listening to her screams on the phone.

Nurse Aisha ran to me and said, "Daksh! Aisha is all fine. She was too weak to carry a baby in her womb. Mostly this does not happen."

But I was still worried. Nurse Aisha asked, "What happened to you? You are not happy."

I went to the Aisha without replied her. I entered her ward, "Aisha! Are you fine?" And I hugged her.

I kissed her head between her eyes.

"Where's our daughter, Aikya!" She asked...

"Her name is Aadab, Aisha!"

"you call her Aadab and I will call Aikya to her." She grinned and we chuckled a bit.

"You seemed disappointed," Aisha said.

"Aisha, I'm in worry."

"What happened?" she asked.

"I got Krishna's call today. And she is in so much pain."

"I knew it, Daksh. That you still love her."

"No that's not I mean."

"Let me complete my words. My love just affected your heart. But you heartily and unconditionally love only to Krishna. Like Osman did with me. My spiritual strength to attract you towards me got less somewhere." She moistens her eyes.

"Aisha! I love you a lot. But, I also have a son. I was not aware of it." I said clearly.

"I wish, I would have died." She said lowering her gaze.

"No, don't say this. I will die if you leave me alone in this world. That was my past." I explained to her.

"Is there anything left in my love for you, if there is? Then I apologize."

I got a call from an unknown number. I received. There was Krishna on the other side

"I reached the airport. I'm coming to you. He gave divorce to me." She said as if nothing happened.

"Did he beat you? And whose number is this? " I asked.

"I came to you then I will explain everything to you."

Aisha said, "When two spirits want to meet and love each other then God unites them and they marry."

"No Aisha, I won't marry her. I only signed you for my whole life."

I got a call from Krishna's number, "Hello! Who's speaking." There was a man on the other side.

I thought that he was her husband. Then he said, "Please cooperate, we are police. There's a dead body of two people. Here I got a phone on the desk. And the last call dialled is your number. You know who was there here.,"

I refused to tell her name and they denied the call. After some time, I got a call again and I heard the news that Krishna murdered his child and her husband. She was travelling in an aeroplane, that crashed on an Island. She is the most evil-hearted girl I ever saw.

I cried a lot but she never did good to me.

When Aisha got to know that she died. She started crying. She was crying because Krishna was my love, and seeing that I lost my love she was so disappointed.

A nurse entered inside the ward, "Sir! Please help me to change her clothes."

"Yes? Me?" I asked, confusedly.

"Of course sir, you are her husband, right?" she reminded me.

"Sister, my husband will change my clothes." She insisted she move outside in an indirect way.

She nodded and moved outside.

I removed her long light blue color gown and helped her put on her clothes. I kissed her forehead and said, "You will be fine soon."

"Don't worry, every soul tastes the death. Either in any way. I know you are still hurting that your love is dying."

"No Aisha, my love is you. I don't forgive those who left me in the middle of the alley."

"Never think like this, forgive her. We seek forgiveness from God and we the human made up of clay don't forgive the sinner of us. So this is not justice. We are keeping hope from God, and we are not forgiving the people of We are keeping hope from God, and we are not forgiving the people of the land." She said.

"You are great Aisha."

"Only God is great. We are the sinner servants of God." Aisha replied.

Doctors came and said, "She is fine. You can take her to the home."

"Thanks to God! And thank you so much, doctors." I shaped the hands.

They gave the discharge to her. I brought Aadab and kept them beside her. She was playing with our cute little daughter.

"Daksh, I still feel that today is my last day in this world." She said suddenly.

"Shut Up Aisha, you should not say these negative words." I quit her.

"Please help me to take inside the bathroom, I want to do ablution(wudu)." Aisha urged.

"But, you're not able to pray Namaz. You're impure, aren't you?"

"But my nifas (bleeding after childbirth) stops. I will do ablution and ghusl (bath).

I held her on both of her shoulders and took her to the bathroom. When she had done with ablution I took back her to the bed. "Please call nurse Aisha," Aisha ordered.

I called her.

Aisha proved gently, "Nurse Aisha, why don't you say that your husband gave you divorce."

"What?" I was surprised.

"How did you know?"

"I'm asking why you hid it from me," Aisha asked, repeatedly.

"You all were already in miserable condition, how can I jump in between with my problems."

"What had happened?" I asked.

"My husband, Afzal. His friends saw both of us at the airport. He started inquiring me about you. And then he started creating doubts in his heart. And those doubts he converted into hate for me. He divorced me. When I was at Ramgadh Hospital. I received a mail. I checked the rug pulled from my feet. I couldn't able to stand on my legs. The divorce paper, I held in my hand.

There was a chair near me, I took a seat.

I pray to God, asking him what I did wrong. You're giving me such a severe penalty."

She started sobbing and hugged Aisha.

"Don't worry. Have patience. You know Nurse Aisha. In the era of Prophet Muhammad (Peace be upon him), there was a woman. Whose husband died. She was so impatiently crying. Then Prophet Muhammad (PBUH) went to her and tried to console her. And he said in the Arabic language, "Indeed, we belong to Allah, and indeed, to Him we return." He said, to have patience, and share one powerful dua with her to get relief from the calamity she faced and will get a better one than the previous.

And you know what, to whom she married. The beautiful person of that era, The one we still know in the world today.

Because of this, the entire universe was created.

The moon stars, the earth, and the beautiful nature swings as soon as they hear his name. "Prophet Muhammad". So, My point is that patience pays sweet. Have patience."

"You are very good Aisha. You have been with me every moment of my life. How will I repay your favour,?"

"Marry Daksh," Aisha replied.

I and nurse Aisha were shocked for a moment.

"What are you saying Aisha, I only love you."

"But, she loves you," Aisha said.

I slowly rolled my eyes towards her. She was embarrassed and worried at the same time.

"I'm going to die. I'm just a temporary guest in this world." Aisha said.

"What are you saying, Aisha." Nurse Aisha interfered, denying her talks in between.

She stood on her legs on the prayer mat. My heartbeats were running rapidly. I hold Aadab in my arms. I was hugging her, and confusedly looking at Nurse Aisha.

Now I understand why someone cares so much.

Nurse Aisha supported me and cared for me so much even in the presence of her husband. Her husband divorced because I was with her. She compromised so much for me. She wanted her love to meet his lover. She wanted my love to win.

I noticed that Aisha had been in prostration for 5 minutes. She has the habit of sleeping in prostration.

When I touched her, she lay on the floor. I called her by her name. Aadab was crying. I called nurse Aisha, and she entered and saw Aisha was on the floor. When Nurse Aisha started waking her up. She stopped calling.

She sat down on the floor. Aadab started crying loudly.

"Inna lillahi wa inna ilayhi rajioon." She uttered.

My tears were silent. Aadab was crying, my legs had no strength to stand for a second. Everything shattered.

Nurse Aisha took Aadab from me, I went close to Aisha.

Put my head on her chest, and kissed her forehead.

"I will miss you, Aisha," I said slowly with a smile on my face.

They took Aisha for the Ghusl (Bath after death). After Ghusl, they shrouded her with Kafan.

"If I died before you, at least pray the funeral prayer for me. I will be happy." I remembered Aisha's words.

I took a bath. And joined them in the funeral prayer. I knew what to utter in prayer. So, I did that the same.

After prayer, everyone started lifting the funeral of Aisha.

Four people took it on their shoulder and then passed it to another four. I took it on my shoulder, it was going to slip from my hand. I had no strength to take her on my shoulder.

And finally, they buried her in the grave. When I returned from the cemetery. I saw the women of the village and other villagers were crying for Aisha. In the love of Aisha.

Nurse Aisha came to me and said, "They loved Aisha so much." She pointed to Siddharth, he was crying silently standing in the corner.

"Look at him. When a servant only loves his God, Then God calls the King of the angels and tells him, This man loves me very much. I do it and you also love him. Then the master of the angels goes and tells all the angels that you all angels have to love that person. Because God likes him very much.

And God puts love for him in the hearts of all the people of the world.

This is the result of love for God." Nurse Aisha said.

She was so fortunate that every person loved her. And this is the blessing.

Aadab was my responsibility right now. But, nurse Aisha used to live at my house in another bedroom. She kept Aadab with her and I slept with Aisha's memory. The time I spent with her was unforgettable. With her memories, I used to sleep. It is included in my daily schedule.

Every night I slept with a grin on my face. Because she's always in my heart. So, remembering her by crying is stupidity.

Ten days had passed. I went to the graveyard.

The morning with dark blue sky and every bird started chirping. I sat beside the grave of Aisha and said, "Aisha, you're always in my heart. Your body is buried in the earth but your spirit is buried in my heart. But, you have to clear your debt. Now you have a Heartache. You will never know, how much my heart is bearing. If I let you open, it will burst out. So, it's better to stay silent and be happy in every situation. Seriously, God put me on a great trial."

I put my head on my knees.

"Daksh, God takes tests to those whom He loves the most.," Aisha said.

I was shocked, I lifted my face and looked. Aisha was in a white colour gown. She came and sat next to me.

"First God put love for that person and then he snatched your loved one from you. When you get shattered then you return to your God. He said, 'Come my servant. Come to me. I will give you calmness, Tranquility, firmness.' And then, When God loves you, you will forget the world's love."

I rolled my eyes and saw her again. But she disappeared.

The challenges I faced in my life were difficult for me. But, indeed, God does not burden a soul beyond what it can bear.

Also, God gave me such a beautiful moment in my life. My phone rang, it was Nurse Aisha's call.

"Daksh, bring milk for Aadab. She's crying because of starving."

I forgot that I also had one daughter in grief of Aisha's death. Nurse Aisha was taking care of her. I got up fast and went to the shop to buy some milk. And when I reached to the home. I saw Aadab was playing.

"I bought milk, feed her," I said.

"Sorry, but she was hungry and you were doing late so I do breastfeed." Nurse Aisha was saying scared.

I went near to her and said, "Thank you so much, Aisha."

"I don't have my child, Daksh, I beg you to give this baby to me," she said begging.

"No, I can't! She's my whole world now. This daughter is a token of my Aisha." Amid the chaos, I remained a tranquil presence, earnestly attempting to elucidate my point to her with a composed demeanour.

I remembered what Aisha had said about me and her, getting married. But I was pressing this thing in my mind. Meanwhile, she said, "Okay, I'm going!"

And she went out taking tears in her eyes.

Aadab was in my hands, she was crying. Anyhow, I put her to sleep.

I put my head on the pillow beside Aadab, Tears were coming out of the lateral commissure of my eye.

I asked her in my mind, 'Why Aisha? You left us alone here. You're the only one who loved me in this deceptive world.' I closed my eyes.

"Aisha!" as I saw her I ran to hug her. And I hugged her.

We were crying looking at both of us.

I asked, "What I did do now? For what sins am I being punished now?" she put her palms on my cheeks, and said, "Not every problem has to be punished for every crime.

Sometimes God tests us. And you will win that test only when you take everything with patience and patience."

"Why he snatched you from me? You left Aadab alone there." I put my head on her shoulder. She was calming me down by running her hand over my face and hair.

"That's why I left you with Aadab. If I ask for you again, God will not deny my prayer. Indeed, He is the Hearer of all." Said Aisha.

"Please Aisha, call me. I can't pray for my death, I know this comes in the sins." I urged.

"Have Patience Daksh. First, ask for forgiveness from Nurse Aisha. She has a spiritual heart, that you hurt."

"Oh God, what I did!" I asked God and cried loudly.

"God forbid, you again have to face the cruelty of this sin."

"Marry her, Marry from Nurse Aisha. Then only she will forgive you." Aisha insisted.

"How can I marry her? I only love you.," I said.

"Don't lie! You only love Krishna. I know! When you heard that Krishna died, so I can feel your heartbeat. Indeed, my part of heart is attached to your heart.

That was my God that put love for me in your heart. Now, Nurse Aisha loves you. She won't express it. Accept her before it's too late."

"Aisha, I forgot everything in your love. I only believe the religion. The religion of Love.

And God, who has multiple names resident in every heart of his servants. I understand, don't break that heart in which God lives. Especially, when God itself has put love for her/his in everyone's heart. That's the spiritual heart. I hurt you, Nurse Aisha, My parents, my friend Sanchit and even Diya. I played with girls, what if any of them had a love for me? You married me after I accepted God. That's the beautiful love for God. That's why God created your heart A Spiritual Heart.

If someone wasn't of true faith, he would have considered you as God."

"Never, we never be able to consider as God. The best of all, and no one beyond him. We humans do not have the slightest love as much as God loves. His love is the same with all his friends.

If we came to know about his love how much he loves you. We will fill the ocean with our tears. Look how much Nurse Aisha is crying in your love. Don't hurt God's servant. Accept her Love." Aisha Said.

"I will accept her with my wholehearted, but my love is only for you," I confessed.

She disappeared.

'That's the love of Spiritual Heart who cares for all heart. And I, the foolish one hurt the Spiritual heart.

You don't need to sin only if you hurt your spiritual heart.

God has appointed the punishment for breaking the hearts of any of His servants.

The heart is God's home, don't break it.

God was even in the heart of a kaafir like me.

Then they have hearts that love God, God likes to live in their hearts.

You will be punished for hurting someone's heart both in the world and in the Hereafter.

'Ae aashiq e ibn e hawwa ya ho tu aashiq e ibn e aadam,

Tu kar Ishq apne khuda ke bando se.

par Yaad rakh,

Teri mohabbat tab tak fareb hai jab tak teri mohabbat me khuda shamil nahi.'

Ibn e hawwa (women)

Ibn e aadam (Men)

_Hamza Salim Khan